SEP 0 5 REC'D

NO LONGER PROPERTY OF
SEATTLE PUBLIC LIBRARY

D0514579

Modern Knitted
SHAWLS
&WRAPS

Modern Knitted
SHAWLS
&WRAPS

35 warm and
stylish designs to
knit, from lacy
shawls to chunky
afghans

Laura Strutt

CICO BOOKS
LONDON NEW YORK

To John and Waffle—the best companions a girl could wish for!

Published in 2017 by CICO Books
An imprint of Ryland Peters & Small Ltd
20-21 Jockey's Fields, London WC1R 4BW
341 E 116th St, New York, NY 10029

www.rylandpeters.com

10 9 8 7 6 5 4 3 2 1

Text © Laura Strutt 2017
Design, illustration, and photography
© CICO Books 2017

The author's moral rights have been asserted.
All rights reserved. No part of this publication may be reproduced, stored in a retrieval system, or transmitted in any form or by any means, electronic, mechanical, photocopying, or otherwise, without the prior permission of the publisher.

A CIP catalog record for this book is available from the Library of Congress and the British Library.

ISBN: 978 1 78249 434 8

Printed in China

Editor: Rachel Atkinson
Pattern checker: Jemima Bicknell
Designer: Alison Fenton
Photographers: Emma Mitchell and Penny Wincer
Stylists: Rob Merrett and Joanna Thornhill
Illustrator: Stephen Dew

Art director: Sally Powell
Production manager: Gordana Simakovic
Publishing manager: Penny Craig
Publisher: Cindy Richards

contents

chapter 1

bright and beautiful 10

chapter 2

warm and rich 52

chapter 3

neutral and natural 80

introduction

As the seasons change, knitted wraps and shawls are fantastic accessories to see you through the transition in true style! There are endless options for color, size, shape, and style, which makes them not only great to add to your own closet but also to give as gifts—there is sure to be something that suits everyone's unique body type and dress sense!

Knitting is a wonderfully creative pastime, and I love to experiment with this medium. The more I knit, the more I learn that the possibilities are endless! With so many different stitches, techniques, and options for customization, there is always something satisfying, challenging, and rewarding waiting to be cast on to your needles. Hopefully this collection of 35 modern knitted shawls and wraps, with their "Make it Yours" suggestions for variations, will provide you with the inspiration to create your own personalized accessories.

This collection is also a fantastic opportunity to try out a few new techniques, from miter squares and brioche knitting, to lace patterns and working in the round. These projects should have something to suit your every knitting mood— whether you are a novice looking for something quick and easy, or you are keen to build your skills and are looking for a more challenging piece. And when you've finished something that you can wear—whether it is for everyday use or for that special occasion—there is a great deal of satisfaction to be had from being able to say, "Yes! I made it myself!"

I hope these patterns for knitted shawls, wraps, afghans, capes, and cowls will spark your imagination, boost your passion for knitting, and allow you to make your very own selection of stunning knitwear which you can be truly proud of!

Happy Knitting!

Laura

before you begin

Knitted shawls are such satisfying projects to make. Not only are you able to try out a range of different techniques and stitch patterns to add to your knitting skills set, you also create a unique handmade accessory to wear with pride! The projects in this book will become great additions to your closet, whether as statement accessories, cozy cover-ups, or simply for a flash of pick-me-up color!

yarn

Knitted shawls can be made from almost any style, thickness, fiber, and finish of yarn. Each will have different properties and lend itself to a distinct look for the finished piece; thicker yarns create a denser fabric and make for wonderfully quick and cozy projects, whilst accessories using lighter weight yarns might take slightly longer to complete, but will create airy designs with more drape and fluidity.

The patterns in this book showcase a range of effects and finishes you can achieve by using different weights, fibers, and styles of yarn—you can even raid your yarn stash to create these makes—just be sure to check the details of the yarn weights, amounts, and gauge (tension) when substituting yarn.

Some of the yarns used in the book are sold in skeins or hanks and it is important to wind these into balls before beginning to knit so as to avoid creating nasty yarn tangles.

It is also very important, particularly for the larger single-color projects such as Purple Reign (page 12) and Ice Queen (page 93), that you have enough yarn before starting. Buying all the required yarn in one go will ensure you have balls or skeins from the same dye lot. Different dye lots can vary considerably in color and changes in dye lots partway through a project will be noticeable.

gauge (tension)

A guide for the gauge (tension) is given with each pattern, and whilst matching this exactly is not as paramount when making accessories, it is important to achieve a gauge as close as possible to the one provided so your finished make has the same look, feel, and size as shown in the photographs. Check your gauge before starting the project and make adjustments by switching the size of the needles—if your gauge is too tight and the stitches in your swatch are smaller than those recommended, try using needles one size larger. Similarly, if your stitches are too large, switch to needles one size smaller and rework the swatch. See page 112 for information on gauge swatches.

Maintaining an even gauge throughout your project is important for a neat and tidy finish as all the stitches will be of a similar size. This is particularly important for projects with feature stitches such as the multiple yarn over stitches in the Waves of Warmth wrap (page 90) where even gauge will create an open repeat pattern.

blocking

Taking time to carefully finish your project will give it a really neat and professional look. Not only does blocking help the fabric lie neatly and to the given measurements, it also opens up the stitches to show off the finer details of your hard work, whether that be lace stitches as seen in Madeira Wine (page 66) or delicate picot edgings seen in Knit a Rainbow (page 14), and Oranges & Lemons (page 48). You can block your finished make either with steam from the iron, or by soaking in lukewarm water before pinning into shape to dry. Remember to check the yarn ball band for specific details on washing the yarn—it's generally advised to hand-wash shawls and wraps. Remember to take care when steaming acrylic and acrylic blend yarns as they can easily stretch out of shape—wet blocking will be a much better option. Cotton and silk yarns can be blocked firmly to encourage the fibers to sit neatly in place. See page 123 for more information on blocking.

lifelines

There is nothing worse for knitters than having to rip back (frog) your work due to a mistake. You can make this process easier to bear by regularly placing lifelines in the knitting, so if you do have to go back a few rows it avoids pulling further back even further than necessary. A lifeline is usually a length of smooth yarn such as cotton, in a lighter weight than the project yarn. When you reach a point where you are sure the stitch count and pattern are correct, use a tapestry needle to thread the lifeline through the stitches on your needle and then continue your knitting. If you need to rip back, remove the knitting from the needle, pull the yarn back to the lifeline which will neatly catch the stitches. Place the stitches back on the needle, continue knitting and repeat the lifeline placement every so often, that way you can be sure the previous section is correct. This method is particularly useful for lace projects such as Rosy Red Wrap (page 78) and brioche knitting such as Sun and Sand (page 99), where mistakes can be tricky to spot and then correct easily.

knitting needles

The patterns in this book indicate the size and type of needles to use with the yarn listed for the project. You can adjust these where necessary to accommodate yarn substitutions and to match the gauge (tension) to that given with the pattern. How you hold the needles and yarn is a matter of preference—there is no right or wrong, as long as you are able to freely move your wrists, hands, and fingers in order to comfortably work neat and even stitches.

Various needle types are used or suggested; straight, circular, and double-pointed needles (DPNs), and each variant has its own benefits. As well as using circular needles and DPNs for working in the round, you will find a circular needle is suggested for working the larger shawls back and forth in rows including A Touch of Pink (page 42) and Feathers and Fans (page 31) among others. Circular needles hold the high volume of stitches and enable you to rest the knitting comfortably on your lap, reducing the stress on your wrists and also allowing you to open up the shawl and see your progress, making mistakes easier to spot!

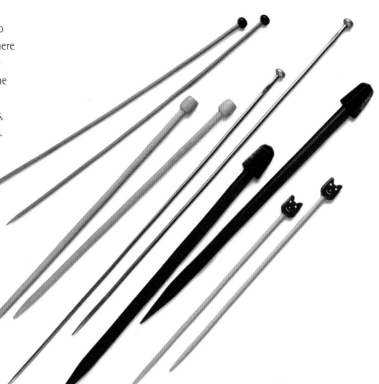

additional equipment

Stitch markers: Used to split a row into defining sections and act as reminders of garter stitch borders or the central point of a row. Many of the patterns in this book include the instruction "place marker" and "work to marker." When you reach the marker simply slip it from the left-hand to right-hand needle so it maintains its correct position and take care when markers are next to yarn overs as they can slip underneath and out of position.

Row counter: This is a small, tubular counter that fits on the end of your knitting needle. You click it round after each completed row.

Tapestry & yarn needles: For securing the ends of the yarn at the start and end of a project and also where color changes occur. For heavier weight yarns, try using a split-eye needle or a crochet hook to secure in the ends neatly.

Sewing needle & thread: Handy to have for securing buttons in place.

Tape measure: Always useful for checking gauge (tension) swatches and finished sizes when blocking. Triangular shawl measurements are usually taken along the long top edge and down the central line.

Rust-proof pins: For holding your project in shape when blocking.

skill levels

Each project includes a star rating as a skill level guide:

Projects incorporating basic stitches, and simple shapes and techniques.

Projects combining different stitches and repetitive stitch patterns, simple color changes, shaping, and finishing.

Projects using a variety of techniques that require more concentration and the ability to "read" your knitting, such as double-sided lace patterns and brioche knitting.

chapter 1

bright and beautiful

purple reign

With its delicate lacy design and jewel-like color, this long, elegant wrap will add a touch of class to your favorite little black dress.

materials

Schachenmayr Catania Fine (100% cotton, approx 180yd/165m per 1¾oz/50g ball) fingering (4ply) weight yarn
  6 balls of shade Phlox 366

US 4 (3.5mm) knitting needles

Tapestry needle

finished measurements

23½in (60cm) wide x 53in (135cm) long

gauge (tension)

2½ repeats of lace pattern (25 sts x 32 rows) to measure 4in (10cm) on US 4 (3.5mm) needles after blocking

abbreviations

See page 126.

make it yours For a completely different look that's perfect for spring or summer, use a white, cream, or other pale neutral shade.

for the wrap

Using US 4 (3.5mm) needles and the long-tail method (see page 114), cast on 141 sts.

Row 1 (RS): K1, *yo, k3, sl1 k2tog psso, k3, yo, k1; rep from * to end.

Row 2 (WS): Purl.

Row 3: K1, *k1, yo, k2, sl1 k2tog psso, k2, yo, k2; rep from * to end.

Row 4: Purl.

Row 5: K1, *k2, yo, k1, sl1 k2tog psso, k1, yo, k3; rep from * to end.

Row 6: Purl.

Row 7: K1, *k3, yo, sl1 k2tog psso, yo, k4; rep from * to end.

Row 8: Purl.

Rows 1-8 set the lace pattern repeat.

Continue repeating rows 1-8 until 149 reps have been worked in total, ending after working a row 8.
Bind (cast) off loosely knitwise.

making up and finishing

Weave in all loose ends and block to measurements.

tip Blocking the finished piece will open up the stitches and show off the delicate lace pattern.

skill level

knit a rainbow

Add a flash of color to your world with this super-sized triangle shawl. Worked from the top down, with blocks of bright shades, this cheerful wrap will brighten your day!

materials

Rowan Cotton Glace (100% cotton, approx 126yd/115m per 1¾oz/50g ball) light worsted (DK) weight yarn

6 balls of shade Ecru 725 (A)

1 ball each of shades:

Poppy 741 (B)

Persimmon 832 (C)

Mineral 856 (D)

Green Slate 844 (E)

Midnight 868 (F)

Garnet 841 (G)

Precious 867 (H)

Aqua 858 (I)

US 4 (3.5mm) circular needle, minimum 48in (120cm) length

Note: The shawl is worked flat in rows but a circular needle is recommended due to the high stitch count.

4 stitch markers

Tapestry needle

finished measurements

92in (233cm) wide x 44in (112cm) deep

gauge (tension)

22 sts x 30 rows to measure 4in (10cm) over stockinette (stocking) stitch on US 4 (3.5mm) needles after blocking

abbreviations

See page 126.

for the shawl

Set-up
Using US 4 (3.5mm) needles and yarn A, cast on 10 sts.

Set-up row 1 (RS): K2, pm, k2, pm, k2, pm, k2, pm, k2. *4 markers placed—slip these as you pass them on all subsequent rows*

Set-up row 2 (WS): K2, p to last 2 sts, k2.

Body of shawl
Row 1 (RS): K2, sm, yo, k to next marker, yo, sm, k2, sm, yo, k to next marker, yo, sm, k2. *4 sts inc*

Row 2 (WS): K2, p to last 2 sts, k2.

Rows 3–124: Rep rows 1 and 2. *258 sts* Break yarn A.

Rainbow stripes
Row 1 (RS): Using yarn B, k2, sm, yo, k to next marker, yo, sm, k2, sm, yo, k to next marker, yo, sm, k2. *4 sts inc*

Row 2 (WS): Knit to end.

Rows 3–12: Rep rows 1–2. Break yarn B. *20 sts inc; 282 sts total*

Row 13: Rejoin yarn A, k2, sm, yo, k to next marker, yo, sm, k2, sm, yo, k to next marker, yo, sm, k2. *286 sts*

Row 14: K2, p to last 2 sts, k2. Break yarn A.

Rows 15–26: Using yarn C, rep rows 1–12. Break yarn C. *310 sts*

Rows 27–28: Using yarn A, rep rows 13–14. Break yarn A. *314 sts*

Rows 29–40: Using yarn D, rep rows 1–12. Break yarn D. *338 sts*

Rows 41–42: Using yarn A, rep rows 13–14. Break yarn A. *342 sts*

Rows 43–54: Using yarn E, rep rows 1–12. Break yarn E. *366 sts*

Rows 55–56: Using yarn A, rep rows 13–14. Break yarn A. *3 70 sts*

Rows 57–68: Using yarn F, rep rows 1–12. Break yarn F. *394 sts*

Rows 69–70: Using yarn A, rep rows 13–14. Break yarn A. *398 sts*

Rows 71–82: Using yarn G, rep rows 1–12. Break yarn G. *422 sts*

Rows 83–84: Using yarn A, rep rows 13–14. Break yarn A. *426 sts*

Rows 85–96: Using yarn H, rep rows 1–12. Break yarn H. *450 sts*

Rows 97–124: Using yarn A, rep rows 13–14 a further 14 times. Break yarn A. *506 sts*

for the picot border

Row 1 (RS): Using yarn I, k2, sm, yo, k to next marker, yo, sm, k2, sm, yo, k to next marker, yo, sm, k2. *510 sts*

Row 2 (WS): Knit to end.

Row 3: K2, remove marker, [yo, k2tog] to next marker, remove marker, k2, remove marker, [yo, k2tog] to next marker, remove marker, k2.

Row 4: Knit to end.

Work picot bind (cast) off as follows: *Using the cable cast-on method (see page 113), cast 2 sts onto LH needle, bind (cast) off 6 sts; rep from * to central spine, cast 2 sts onto LH needle, bind (cast) off 5 sts to position next picot point at the tip of shawl, cast 2 sts onto LH needle, bind (cast) off 5 sts to mirror other side, **cast 2 sts onto LH needle, bind (cast) off 6 sts; rep from ** to end. Break yarn and pull through remaining st.

making up and finishing
Weave in all loose ends and block to measurements, taking time to pin out the picot points.

---

make it yours For a smoother, less textured finish, work the garter stitch rainbow stripes in stockinette (stocking) stitch.

---

tip Work the picot border bind (cast) off loosely to add more definition to the points. If the stitches are too tight, move up a needle size for the bind- (cast-) off row.

---

tips The shawl is increased on right-side knit rows at each end of the row and each side of the central spine. Use stitch markers to keep track of where to make the increases but ensure they don't slip under the yarn overs.

When changing shades, you will break one yarn and join in the next specified color. Leave a tail of at least 4in (10cm) of the previous color when breaking the yarn, to weave in later.

sunshine on a rainy day

Keep cozy with this big, button-up capelet. Accented with a fancy crochet border, it's a chunky knit that will see you from fall through to winter in true style.

materials

Rowan Big Wool (100% wool, approx 87yd/80m per 3½oz/100g ball) super-bulky (super-chunky) weight yarn
   3 balls of shade Sun 68 (A)

Rowan Brushed Fleece (65% wool, 30% alpaca, 5% polyamide, approx 115yd/105m per 1¾oz/50g ball) super-bulky (super-chunky) weight yarn
   2 balls of shade Cove 251 (B)

US 15 (10mm) knitting needles

US J/10 (6mm) crochet hook

Tapestry needle

2 x 2¼in (6cm) buttons

finished measurements

18in (45cm) wide x 49in (124cm) long

gauge (tension)

8 sts x 14 rows to measure 4in (10cm) over seed (moss) stitch on US 15 (10mm) needles after blocking

abbreviations

See page 126.

pattern note

The border is worked in crochet. US and UK crochet terms differ and the same term is used for different stitches. Both versions have been given here.

make it yours You could use bright, bold-colored buttons for more contrast.

tip To keep track when working in seed (moss) stitch pattern, work purl stitches on the stitches you knitted in the previous row, and vice versa.

tip When weaving in ends, you may find super-bulky (super-chunky) yarns don't fit through the eye of a tapestry needle; try using a small crochet hook to secure them instead.

for the capelet

Using US 15 (10mm) needles and yarn A, cast on 30 sts.

Row 1 (RS): *K1, p1; rep from * to end.

Row 2 (WS): *P1, k1; rep from * to end

Rows 1–2 set seed (moss) stitch pattern.

Continue repeating rows 1–2 until piece measures 44½in (113cm) from cast-on edge, ending with a WS row.

Next row (RS)(buttonholes): Work 6 sts in pattern, bind (cast) off next 3 sts, pattern to last 9 sts, bind (cast) off next 3 sts, pattern to end.

Next row (WS)(buttonholes): Work in pattern to bound (cast) off sts, using the backward loop method (see page 113), cast on 3 sts, work 12 sts in pattern, using the backward loop method, cast on 3 sts, pattern to end. Rep rows 1–2 twice more.

Bind (cast) off knitwise.

for the crochet border

Using US J/10 (6mm) crochet hook and with RS facing, join yarn B in any edge stitch.

Round 1: Work 1ch (does not count as st throughout), then 1sc (UK: 1dc) in each stitch and row end around the shawl, working [1sc, 1ch, 1sc] (UK: [1dc, 1ch, 1dc]) in each corner and joining the round with sl st in first sc (UK: first dc), ensuring the total number of sc (UK: dc) is divisible by 4.

Round 2: 1ch, *1sc (UK: 1dc), 3ch, skip (miss) 3 sts; rep from * to end of round, join with sl st in first sc (UK: first dc).

Round 3: 1ch, *1sc in sc, 6dc in chain space (UK: *1dc in dc, 6tr in chain space); rep from * to end of round, join with sl st in first sc (UK: first dc). Fasten off.

making up and finishing

Weave in all loose ends and block to measurements.

Fold the wrap so the buttonhole end is at right angles to the other short end and sew the buttons in place to correspond to the buttonholes (see photos for reference).

turquoise triangles

Working with a combination of knit and purl stitches, this rectangular wrap features a wonderful geometric motif.

materials

Rowan Pure Wool Worsted (100% wool, approx 218yd/200m per 3½oz/100g ball) worsted (Aran) weight yarn
- 3 balls of shade Azure 138 (A)
- 1 ball of shade Breton 147 (B)

US 7 (4.5mm) knitting needles

US H/8 (5mm) crochet hook

2 stitch markers

Tapestry needle

finished measurements

18in (45cm) wide x 55in (140cm) long

gauge (tension)

15 sts x 25 rows to measure 4in (10cm) over triangle stitch pattern on US 7 (4.5mm) needles after blocking.

abbreviations

See page 126.

make it yours Add a striped pattern by alternating the colors of yarn after every knitted pattern repeat.

for the wrap

Bottom edge

Using yarn A and US 7 (4.5mm) needles, cast on 63 sts.
Knit 2 rows.

Next row: K3, pm, k to last 3 sts, pm, k3. *2 markers placed*

Main body

Row 1 (RS): K3, sm, k7, p1, [k13, p1] to last 10 sts, k7, sm, k3.

Row 2 (WS and all following WS rows): K3, sm, p to marker, sm, k3.

Row 3: K3, sm, k6, p3, [k11, p3] to last 9 sts, k6, sm, k3.

Row 5: K3, sm, k5, p5, [k9, p5] to last 8 sts, k5, sm, k3.

Row 7: K3, sm, k4, p7, [k7, p7] to last 7 sts, k4, sm, k3.

Row 9: K3, sm, k3, p9, [k5, p9] to last 6 sts, k3, sm, k3.

Row 11: K3, sm, k2, p11, [k3, p11] to last 5 sts, k2, sm, k3.

Row 13: K3, sm, k1, [p13, k1] to marker, sm, k3.

Row 15: K3, sm, p1, [k13, p1] to marker, sm, k3.

Row 17: K3, sm, p2, k11, [p3, k11] to last 5 sts, p2, sm, k3.

Row 19: K3, sm, p3, k9, [p5, k9] to last 6 sts, p3, sm, k3.

Row 21: K3, sm, p4, k7, [p7, k7] to last 7 sts, p4, sm, k3.

Row 23: K3, sm, p5, k5, [p9, k5] to last 8 sts, p5, sm, k3.

Row 25: K3, sm, p6, k3, [p11, k3] to last 9 sts, p6, sm, k3.

Row 27: K3, sm, p7, k1, [p13, k1] to last 10 sts, p7, sm, k3.

Row 28 (WS): K3, sm, p to marker, sm, k3.

Rep rows 1–28 a further 11 times.

Top edge

Knit 3 rows.
Bind (cast) off.

for the crochet border

With RS facing, using US H/8 (5mm), join yarn B in any row end.

Round 1: 1ch then 1sc (UK: 1dc) in each st and row end around the shawl, working 2sc (UK: 2dc) in each corner and joining the round with a sl st in first sc (UK: dc).

Rounds 2–3: Rep round 1. Fasten off.

making up and finishing

Weave in all loose ends and block to measurements.

tip The two stitch markers act as a reminder to work the first and last 3 stitches of every row as "knit" to create a garter stitch border.

tip When taking a break from your knitting make a note of where you are in the pattern repeat to make for a quick restart when you return.

pretty pastels

This classic shoulder shawl, worked in a silk blend yarn, will make a lovely addition to a sweet summer outfit.

materials
Cascade Heritage Silk Paints (85% merino wool, 15% silk, 437yd/399m per 3½oz/100g skein) fingering (4ply) weight yarn
  2 skeins of shade Dried Flowers 9779

US 6 (4mm) circular needle, minimum 40in (100cm) length

Note: The shawl is worked flat in rows but a circular needle is recommended due to the high stitch count.

6 stitch markers

Tapestry needle

finished measurements
59in (150cm) along top edge x 23in (58cm) deep

gauge (tension)
22 sts x 29 rows to measure 4in (10cm) over stockinette (stocking) stitch on US 6 (4mm) needles after blocking

abbreviations
See page 126.

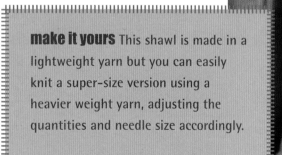

make it yours This shawl is made in a lightweight yarn but you can easily knit a super-size version using a heavier weight yarn, adjusting the quantities and needle size accordingly.

bright and beautiful

for the shawl

Using US 6 (4mm) needles, cast on 3 sts.

Row 1 (WS): K1, yo, k1, yo, k1. *5 sts*

Row 2 (RS): Knit.

Row 3: K1, yo, k3, yo, k1. *7 sts*

Row 4: Knit.

Row 5: K1, yo, k5, yo, k1. *9 sts*

Row 6: K3, [yo, k1] to last 3 sts, yo, k3. *13 sts*

Row 7: K3, p to last 3 sts, k3.

Row 8: Knit.

Row 9: K3, p to last 3 sts, k3.

Row 10: K3, yo, [k1, yo, pm, k1, pm, yo] 3 times, k1, yo, k3. *21 sts; 6 markers placed—slip these as you pass them on all subsequent rows*

Row 11: K3, p to last 3 sts, k3.

Row 12: Knit.

Row 13: K3, p to last 3 sts, k3.

Row 14: K3, yo, [k to marker, yo, sm, k1, sm, yo] 3 times, k to last 3 sts, yo, k3. *8 sts inc*

Rows 15–166: Rep rows 11–14. *333 sts*

Rows 167–170: Knit.

Bind (cast) off loosely knitwise.

making up and finishing

Weave in all ends and block to measurements taking care to shape the shawl into a curve.

tip The stitch markers are used to indicate yarn over (yo) increases and you may find that the stitch markers occasionally slip under the yarn overs which can throw the increase pattern off. If you suspect this has happened, work back a row or slip the stitch marker under the yarn over and into its correct position.

make it yours Work in two solid shades of yarn, switching halfway through, after working row 86, to create a modern version with high impact.

peaches and cream

Play up the ombré effect of the yarns with the delicate eyelet detail featured in this shawl, which is ideal for knitters who are new to lace patterns!

materials

Cascade Ultra Pima (100% cotton, approx 218yd/200m per 3½oz/100g skein) light worsted (DK) weight yarn

  1 skein each of shades:
  Natural 3718 (A)
  White Peach 3753 (B)
  Coral 3752 (C)
  2 skeins of shade Deep Coral 3767   (D)

US 6 (4mm) circular needle, minimum 40in (100cm) length

Note: The shawl is worked flat in rows but a circular needle is recommended due to the high stitch count.

2 stitch markers

Tapestry needle

finished measurements

88in (224cm) wide x 39½in (100cm) deep

gauge (tension)

20 sts x 28 rows to measure 4in (10cm) over stockinette (stocking) stitch on US 6 (4mm) needles after blocking

abbreviations

See page 126.

tip The yarn used for this design is supplied in skeins. Be sure to wind the yarn into balls before starting your project, so as to avoid nasty tangles as you knit.

tip Blocking your shawl will open up the eyelets, make the delicate lace pattern more visible, and give a neat and professional finish to the project.

make it yours Cotton yarns are lovely for late spring and summer wear, but this design will work just as well in a wool or wool blend for the colder seasons.

This shawl will look great in ombré shades of any color, but you could always work in stripes of your four favorite shades if preferred.

for the shawl

Using yarn A and US 6 (4mm) needles, cast on 5 sts.

Set-up row 1 (RS): K1, yo, k1, yo, pm, k1, pm, yo, k1, yo, k1. *9 sts; 2 markers placed—slip these as you pass them on all subsequent rows*

Set-up row 2 (WS): Purl.

Row 1 (RS): K1, yo, k to marker, yo, sm, k1, sm, yo, k to last st, yo, k1. *4 sts inc*

Row 2 (WS): Purl.

Rows 3–94: Rep rows 1–2. *197 sts*

Change to yarn B.

Row 95 (RS)(Eyelet row): K1, yo, [k2tog, yo] to 1 st before marker, k1, yo, sm, k1, sm, yo, k1, [yo, k2tog] to last st, yo, k1. *4 sts inc*

Row 96 (WS): Purl.

Row 97: K1, yo, k to marker, yo, sm, k1, sm, yo, k to last st, yo, k1. *4 sts inc*

Row 98: Purl.

Rows 99–102: Rep rows 97–98 twice more. *8 sts inc; 213 sts total*

Rep rows 95–102 a further 3 times. *261 sts*

Change to yarn C and rep rows 95–102 a total of 4 times. *325 sts*

Change to yarn D and rep rows 95–102 a total of 4 times. *389 sts*

Border

Continue in yarn D.

Row 1 (RS)(Eyelet row): K1, yo, [k2tog, yo] to 1 st before marker, k1, yo, sm, k1, sm, yo, k1, [yo, k2tog] to last st, yo, k1. *4 sts inc*

Row 2 (WS): Purl.

Rep rows 1–2 a further 5 times. *413 sts*

Bind (cast) off knitwise.

making up and finishing

Weave in all ends and block to measurements.

feathers and fans

This wrap combines a traditional lace stitch with a modern, long color change yarn for a contemporary look. Feather and fan stitch pattern is a simple repeat of increasing and decreasing stitches, making it ideal for adventurous beginners.

materials

Noro Kureopatora (100% wool, approx 295yd/270m per 3½oz/100g ball) worsted (Aran) weight yarn
  4 balls of shade 1011

US 8 (5mm) circular needle, minimum 40in (100cm) length

Note: The wrap is worked flat in rows but a circular needle is recommended due to the high stitch count.

Tapestry needle

finished measurements

19½in (50cm) wide x 79in (200cm) long

gauge (tension)

18 sts x 26 rows to measure 4in (10cm) over feather and fan stitch on US 8 (5mm) needles after blocking

abbreviations

See page 126.

bright and beautiful

for the wrap

Using US 8 (5mm) needles, loosely cast on 360 sts.

Row 1 (RS): Knit.

Row 2 (WS): Purl.

Row 3: *[K2tog] 3 times, [yo, k1] 6 times, [k2tog] 3 times; rep from * to end.

Row 4: Knit.

Rows 1–4 set feather and fan pattern.

Rep rows 1–4 until piece measures 19½in (50cm) from cast-on edge ending with WS row 4 of pattern.

Bind (cast) off knitwise.

making up and finishing

Weave in all loose ends and block to measurements taking care to pin out the scalloped edges.

make it yours This wrap is knitted widthwise, starting from the longest edge. To adjust the length, cast on more or fewer stitches in a multiple of 18 and to make it wider or narrower, vary the number of 4-row repeats. Remember to adjust the yarn quantity!

tips If you are worried about losing your place, position stitch markers after each 18-stitch repeat across the row so that you know where they begin and end.

Larger pieces like this can be worked more easily on a circular needle where the weight of the project is better supported on the cable at the center of the needle.

coral formations

This pretty triangular shawl, knitted from the top down, features a number of different stitch combinations to create a dramatic textured finish.

materials

Brown Sheep Company Lamb's Pride Worsted (85% wool, 15% mohair, approx 190yd/173m per 4oz/113g ball) worsted (Aran) weight yarn

  3 balls of shade Deep Coral M159

US 8 (5mm) circular needle, minimum 40in (100cm) length

Note: The shawl is worked flat in rows but a circular needle is recommended due to the high stitch count.

2 stitch markers

Tapestry needle

finished measurements

52in (132cm) wide x 25½in (65cm) deep

gauge (tension)

16 sts x 26 rows to measure 4in (10cm) over stockinette (stocking) stitch on US 8 (5mm) needles after blocking

abbreviations

See page 126.

for the shawl

Using US 8 (5mm) needles, cast on 5 sts.
Set-up row 1 (RS): K2, yo, pm, k1, pm, yo, k2. *7 sts; 2 markers placed–slip these as you pass them on all subsequent rows*
Set-up row 2 (WS): K2, p to last 2 sts, k2.

Stockinette (stocking) stitch section

Row 1 (RS): K2, yo, k to marker, yo, sm, k1, sm, yo, k to last 2 sts, yo, k2. *4 sts inc*
Row 2 (WS): K2, p to last 2 sts, k2.
Rows 3–40: Rep rows 1–2. *87 sts*

tip This shawl is worked downward from the center of the upper neckline edge, increasing by four stitches—two at the spine and one at each end—every right-side row to create the triangular shape.

Reverse stockinette (stocking) stitch band

Row 41 (RS): K2, yo, p to marker, yo, sm, k1, sm, yo, p to last 2 sts, yo, k2. *4 sts inc*

Row 42 (WS): Knit, slipping markers as you pass them.

Row 43: K2, yo, p to marker, yo, sm, k1, sm, yo, p to last 2 sts, yo, k2. *4 sts inc; 95 sts total*

Row 44: K2, p to last 2 sts, k2.

Twisted rib section

Row 45 (RS): K2, yo, [k1tbl, p1] to 1 st before marker, k1tbl, yo, sm, k1, sm, yo, [k1tbl, p1] to last 3 sts, k1tbl, yo, k2. *4 sts inc*

Row 46 (WS): K2, [k1tbl, p1] to 1 st before marker, k1tbl, sm, p1, sm, [k1tbl, p1] to last 3 sts, k1tbl, k2.

Row 47: K2, yo, [p1, k1tbl] to 1 st before marker, p1, yo, sm, k1, sm, yo, [p1, k1tbl] to last 3 sts, p1, yo, k2. *4 sts inc*

Row 48: K2, [p1, k1tbl] to 1 st before marker, p1, sm, p1, sm, [p1, k1tbl] to last 3 sts, p1, k2.

Rows 49–53: Rep rows 45-48 once more, then rep row 45 again. *12 sts inc; 115 sts total*

Row 54: K2, p to last 2 sts, k2.

Reverse stockinette (stocking) stitch band

Rows 55-58: Rep rows 41-44. *123 sts total*

Moss stitch section

Row 59 (RS): K2, yo, [k1, p1] to 1 st before marker, k1, yo, sm, k1, sm, yo, k1, [p1, k1] to last 2 sts, yo, k2. *4 sts inc*

Row 60 (WS): K2, [p1, k1] to 1 st before marker, p1, sm, p1, sm, p1, [k1, p1] to last 2 sts, k2.

Row 61: K2, yo, [p1, k1] to 1 st before marker, p1, yo, sm, k1, sm, yo, p1, [k1, p1] to last 2 sts, yo, k2. *4 sts inc*

Row 62: K2, [k1, p1] to 1 st before marker, k1, sm, p1, sm, k1, [p1, k1] to last 2 sts, k2.

Rows 63–67: Rep rows 59-62 once more then rep row 59 again. *12 sts inc; 143 sts total*

Row 68: K2, p to last 2 sts, k2.

Reverse stockinette (stocking) stitch band

Rows 69–72: Rep rows 41-44. *8 sts inc; 151 sts total*

Honeycomb section

Note: When working this section, slip sts purlwise with yarn in back.

Row 73 (RS): K2, yo, k to marker, yo, sm, k1, sm, yo, k to last 2 sts, k2. *4 sts inc*

Row 74 (WS): K2, [k1, sl1] to 1 st before marker, k1, sm, p1, sm, k1, [sl1, k1] to last 2 sts, k2.

Row 75 (RS): K2, yo, k to marker, yo, sm, k1, sm, yo, k to last 2 sts, k2. *4 sts inc*

Rows 76–81: Rep rows 74-75. *12 sts inc; 171 sts total*

Row 82: K2, p to last 2 sts, k2.

Reverse stockinette (stocking) stitch band

Rows 83–86: Rep rows 41-44. *8 sts inc; 179 sts total*

Lace openwork section

Row 87 (RS): K2, yo, [k2tog, yo] to 1 st before marker, k1, yo, sm, k1, sm, yo, k1, [yo, ssk] to last 2 sts, yo, k2. *4 sts inc*

Row 88 (WS): K2, p to last 2 sts, k2.

Rows 89–96: Rep rows 87-88. *16 sts inc; 199 sts total*

Reverse stockinette (stocking) stitch band

Rows 97–100: Rep rows 41–44. *8 sts inc; 207 sts total*

Stockinette (stocking) stitch section

Row 101 (RS): K2, yo, k to marker, yo, sm, k1, sm, yo, k to last 2 sts, yo, k2. *4 sts inc*

Row 102 (WS): K2, p to last 2 sts, k2.

Rows 103–116: Rep rows 101-102. *28 sts inc; 239 sts*

Reverse stockinette (stocking) stitch band

Rows 117–120: Rep rows 41-44. *8 sts inc; 247 sts total*

Bind (cast) off loosely knitwise.

making up and finishing

Weave in all loose ends and block to measurements.

tip You may find that the stitch markers slip under the yarn overs (yo) worked next to them. Ensure you only ever have one stitch in between the two central spine markers.

make it yours Increase the size of the shawl and create a super-size design by repeating the textured pattern once more, but remember to increase the yarn quantity to accommodate any additional rows.

sherbet swirl

This long, distinctive, vortex-shaped shawl features a saw-tooth edge created by working decorative yarn over increases combined with regular bind (cast) offs. It is a simple, satisfying knit and a great canvas for playing with color and stripes.

materials

Cascade Ultra Pima (100% cotton, approx 218yd/200m per 3½oz/100g skein) light worsted (DK) weight yarn

  1 skein of shade Natural 3718 (A)
  1 skein of shade Pink Rose 3776 (B)
  1 skein of shade Sage 3720 (C)
  1 skein of shade White Peach 3753 (D)
  1 skein of shade Ginseng 3721 (E)

US 8 (5mm) knitting needles

Tapestry needle

finished measurements

10in (26cm) wide at widest point x 102in (260cm) long

gauge (tension)

22 sts x 26 rows to measure 4in (10cm) over garter stitch on US 8 (5mm) needles after blocking

abbreviations

See page 126.

make it yours Wear this shawl scarf style or wrapped multiple times around your shoulders and neck—it looks great secured with a statement shawl pin.

for the shawl

Set-up

Using US 8 (5mm) needles and yarn A, cast on 3 sts.

Set-up row 1 (WS): Knit.

Set-up row 2 (RS): K1, yo, k to end. *4 sts*

Set-up row 3: Knit.

Set-up row 4: K1, yo, k to end. *5 sts*

Set-up row 5: Knit.

Set-up row 6: K1, yo, k to end. *6 sts*

Set-up row 7: Knit.

Set-up row 8: K1, yo, k to end. *7 sts*

Set-up row 9: Bind (cast) off 3 sts, k to end. *4 sts*

Establish saw-tooth repeat

Note: You will now work an 8-row repeat throughout, increasing 4 stitches then binding (casting) off 3 stitches to create the saw-tooth edging and to give a total increase of 1 stitch per repeat that gradually widens the shawl.

Row 1 (RS): K1, yo, k to end. *1 st inc*

Row 2 (WS): Knit.

Rows 3–6: Rep rows 1–2. *2 sts inc*

Row 7: K1, yo, k to end. *1 st inc*

Row 8: Bind (cast) off 3 sts, k to end. *3 sts dec*

Rows 1–8 set the saw-tooth repeat.

Rep rows 1–8 twice more. *7 sts*

Using yarn B, rep rows 1–8 once. *8 sts*

Using yarn A, rep rows 1–8 four times. *12 sts*

Using yarn C, rep rows 1–8 once. *13 sts*

Using yarn A, rep rows 1–8 four times. *17 sts*

Using yarn D, rep rows 1–8 once. *18 sts*

Using yarn A, rep rows 1–8 four times. *22 sts*

Using yarn E, rep rows 1–8 once. *23 sts*

> **tip** Garter stitch makes this shawl reversible but to keep track of the designated right-side (RS) and wrong-side (WS) rows in the pattern, place a locking stitch marker into the right-side of the fabric so you can easily keep track of which row you are working.

> **make it yours** The repetitive nature of the shaping for this shawl means you can work in your own pattern for stripes, ombré, and color-blocks, or use a variegated yarn throughout for a completely different look.

Using yarn A, rep rows 1–8 twice. *25 sts*

Using yarn B, rep rows 1–8 once. *26 sts*

Using yarn A, rep rows 1–8 twice. *28 sts*

Using yarn C, rep rows 1–8 once. *29 sts*

Using yarn A, rep rows 1–8 twice. *31 sts*

Using yarn D, rep rows 1–8 once. *32 sts*

Using yarn A, rep rows 1–8 twice. *34 sts*

Using yarn E, rep rows 1–8 once. *35 sts*

Using yarn A, rep rows 1–8 once. *36 sts*

Using yarn B, rep rows 1–8 twice. *38 sts*

Using yarn A, rep rows 1–8 once. *39 sts*

Using yarn C, rep rows 1–8 twice. *41 sts*

Using yarn A, rep rows 1–8 once. *42 sts*

Using yarn D, rep rows 1–8 twice. *44 sts*

Using yarn A, rep rows 1–8 once. *45 sts*

Using yarn E, rep rows 1–8 twice. *47 sts*

Using yarn A, rep rows 1–8 once. *48 sts*

Using yarn B, rep rows 1–8 four times. *52 sts*

Using yarn A, rep rows 1–8 once. *53 sts*

Using yarn C, rep rows 1–8 four times. *57 sts*

Using yarn A, rep rows 1–8 once. *58 sts*

Using yarn D, rep rows 1–8 four times. *62 sts*

Using yarn A, rep rows 1–8 once. *63 sts*

Using yarn E, rep rows 1–8 four times. *67 sts*

Bind (cast) off all sts knitwise.

making up and finishing

Weave in all loose ends and block to measurements.

a touch of pink

Wrap yourself up in this striking monochrome triangular shawl, incorporating a horseshoe lace border worked in a bright contrasting shade to give your finished accessory a pop of color!

materials

Rowan Handknit Cotton (100% cotton, approx 92yd/85m per 1¾oz/50g ball) worsted (Aran) weight yarn

  3 balls of shade Bleached 263 (A)
  2 balls of shade Slate 347 (B)
  1 ball of shade Flamingo 368 (C)

US 8 (5mm) circular needle, minimum 40in (100cm) length

Note: The shawl is worked flat in rows but a circular needle is recommended due to the high stitch count.

2 stitch markers

Tapestry needle

finished measurements

66in (168cm) wide x 27in (68cm) deep to the point of the triangle

gauge (tension)

15 sts x 22 rows to measure 4in (10cm) over stockinette (stocking) stitch on US 8 (5mm) needles after blocking

abbreviations

See page 126.

tip Using the specified cable cast-on method for the picot bind (cast) off keeps the stitches neat and even, creating uniform points.

make it yours Play with color combinations for the stripes and border. Go bold, neutral, multi-colored, or knit up an ombré design by working with gradient tones of the same shade.

tip The stripes in the main body of this shawl leave a lot of ends to weave in! You can either carry the yarn loosely up the side of the work (which is most economical) or weave in the ends as you go to save time after binding (casting) off.

for the shawl

Body of shawl

Using US 8 (5mm) needles and yarn A, cast on 10 sts.
Row 1 (RS): K4, pm, k2, pm, k4. *2 markers placed—slip these as you pass them on all subsequent rows*
Row 2 (WS): K2, p to last 2 sts, k2.
Row 3: K2, yo, k to marker, yo, sm, k2, sm, yo, k to last 2 sts, yo, k2. *4 sts inc*
Row 4: K2, p to last 2 sts, k2.
Rows 5–52: Rep rows 3–4. *110 sts*

Striped section

Rows 53–54: Change to yarn B and rep rows 3–4. *114 sts*
Rows 55–56: Change to yarn A and rep rows 3–4. *118 sts*
Rows 57–116: Rep rows 53–56. *238 sts*
Rows 117–118: Change to yarn B and rep rows 3–4. *242 sts*

Border

Change to yarn C.
Row 1 (RS): *K1, yo, k4, sl2 k1 psso, k4, yo; rep from * to marker, sm, k2, sm, **yo, k4, sl2 k1 psso, k4, yo, k1; rep from ** to end.
Row 2 (WS): K2, p to last 2 sts, k2.
Row 3: *K2, yo, k3, sl2 k1 psso, k3, yo, k1; rep from * to marker, sm, k2, sm, **k1, yo, k3, sl2 k1 psso, k3, yo, k2; rep from ** to end.
Row 4: K2, p to last 2 sts, k2.
Row 5: *K3, yo, k2, sl2 k1 psso, k2, yo, k2; rep from * to marker, sm, k2, sm, **k2, yo, k2, sl2 k1 psso, k2, yo, k3; rep from ** to end.
Row 6: K2, p to last 2 sts, k2.
Row 7: *K4, yo, k1, sl2 k1 psso, k1, yo, k3; rep from * to marker, sm, k2, sm, **k3, yo, k1, sl2 k1 psso, k1, yo, k4; rep from ** to end.
Row 8: K2, p to last 2 sts, k2.
Row 9: *K5, yo, sl2 k1 psso, yo, k4; rep from from * to marker, sm, k2, sm, **k4, yo, sl2 k1 psso, yo, k5; rep from ** to end.
Row 10: K2, p to last 2 sts, k2
Bind (cast) off loosely knitwise.

making up and finishing

Weave in all loose ends and block to measurements.

catherine wheel

Worked from the center outward with spiraling increases, this large circular shawl is much like a pinwheel. It's soothing to make and wonderful to wrap both yourself and baby up in.

materials

Cascade Heritage Solids (75% wool, 25% nylon, approx 437yd/400m per 3½oz/100g skein) fingering (4ply) weight yarn
  1 skein of shade Placid Blue 5713 (A)

Cascade Heritage Prints (75% wool, 25% nylon, approx 437yd/400m per 3½oz/100g skein) fingering (4ply) weight yarn
  1 skein of shade Iridescence 50 (B)

US 5 (3.75mm) DPNs (double-pointed needles)

US 5 (3.75mm) circular needles, 16in (40cm), 24in (60cm), and 32in (80cm) lengths

8 stitch markers—1 in a different color/style to the other 7

Tapestry needle

finished measurements

36in (91cm) diameter

gauge (tension)

18 sts x 28 rows to measure 4in (10cm) over stockinette (stocking) stitch on US 5 (3.75mm) needles

abbreviations

See page 126.

for the shawl

Using US 5 (3.75mm) DPNs and yarn A, cast on 8 sts. Join for working in the round, taking care not to twist the sts and place the unique stitch marker to indicate beginning of round.

Round 1: [K1, yo, pm] 8 times noting that the eighth marker will be the beginning-of-round marker and is already placed. *16 sts*
Round 2: Knit.
Round 3: [K to marker, yo, sm] 8 times. *8 sts inc*
Round 4: Knit.
Rounds 5–90: Rep rounds 3–4. *368 sts*

Eyelet border
Change to yarn B.
Round 1: *[Yo, k2tog] to marker, yo, sm; rep from * to end. *8 sts inc*
Round 2: Knit.
Round 3: K1, [yo, k2tog] to marker, yo, sm; rep from * to end. *8 sts inc*
Round 4: Knit.
Rounds 5–12: Rep rounds 1–4. *416 sts*
Round 13: [K to marker, yo, sm] 8 times. *8 sts inc*
Round 14: Knit.
Rounds 15–34: Rep rounds 13–14. *504 sts*

For the picot bind (cast) off
Using the cable cast-on method (see page 113), cast on 2 sts, immediately bind (cast) off 4 sts, *slip st on RH needle back to LH needle, cable cast on 2 sts, bind (cast) off 4 sts; rep from * to end. Fasten off.

making up and finishing

Weave in all loose ends and block in a circle to measurements, taking time to pin out the picot points.

make it yours Stripes, color-blocking, or richly variegated yarns will all work well for this shawl—you could even work in different textures, maybe a smooth silk blend yarn for the center and a fluffy mohair for the border!

tips Cast on with the double-pointed needles, changing to circular needles when there are sufficient stitches, then gradually switch up to the longer lengths as the stitch count and circumference increases.

This shawl is shaped by working an 8-stitch increase every other round, creating an octagon which is then blocked into a circle.

oranges and lemons

This shawl has three spines—where the decorative yarn over increases are placed—and is worked outward from the top center to create an intersected square shape that will sit neatly over your shoulders.

materials

Berroco Boboli Lace (42% wool, 35% acrylic, 23% viscose, approx 350yd/320m per 3½oz/100g ball) fingering (4ply) weight yarn
  2 balls of shade Coral Reef 4385

US 9 (5.5mm) circular needle, minimum 40in (100cm) length

Note: The shawl is worked flat in rows but a circular needle is recommended due to the high stitch count.

3 stitch markers

Tapestry needle

finished measurements

36in (91cm) square

gauge (tension)

12 sts x 24 rows to measure 4in (10cm) over garter stitch on US 9 (5.5mm) needles after blocking

abbreviations

See page 126.

make it yours This simple square design can be easily customized with the addition of solid colored stripes in a similar weight yarn.

tips The shape of this shawl is created with a series of 8-stitch increases worked every other row. There are five increase points; one at each edge and three in the main body of the shawl, indicated by stitch markers. Increases are worked with a yarn over (yo) to create a decorative lace hole and there is always one knitted stitch between the two yarn overs at the three increase points in the main body. You will soon see the increase lines appearing.

If you find yourself getting in a tangle with the circular needle, start the shawl on a set of long straight knitting needles and change over to the circular needle once the pattern is established.

for the shawl

Using US 9 (5.5mm) needles, cast on 3 sts.

Row 1 (RS): *K1, yo; rep from * to last st, k1. *5 sts*

Row 2 (WS): Knit.

Row 3: *K1, yo; rep from * to last st, k1. *9 sts*

Row 4: Knit.

Row 5: *[K1, yo] twice, pm; rep from * twice more, [k1, yo] twice, k1. *17 sts; 3 markers placed—slip these as you pass them on all subsequent rows*

Row 6: Knit.

Row 7: K1, yo, *k to marker, yo, sm, k1, yo; rep from * twice more, k to last st, yo, k1. *8 sts inc*

Rows 8–94: Rep rows 6–7, ending with row 6. *369 sts*

Row 95: K1, yo, *k to marker, yo, sm, k1, yo; rep from * twice more, k to last st, yo, k1. *8 sts inc*

Row 96 (WS): Purl.

Rows 97–108: Rep rows 95–96. *425 sts*

For the picot bind (cast) off

Using the cable cast-on method (see page 113), cast on 2 sts, immediately bind (cast) off 4 sts, *slip st on RH needle back to LH needle, cable cast on 2 sts, bind (cast) off 4 sts; rep from * to end. Fasten off.

making up and finishing

Weave in all loose ends and block to measurements, taking time to pin out the picot points.

never-ending color

This clever wrap is worked in the round, however, using Cat Bordhi's unique twisting technique for the cast on (see page 114) means that you are working both sides of the cast-on row on one complete round. This wrap is as impressive to knit as it is to wear and it will all become clear as you work.

materials
Noro Silk Garden (45% silk, 45% mohair, 10% wool, approx 110yd/100m per 1¾oz/50g ball) worsted (Aran) weight yarn
   3 balls of shade 415

US 10 (6mm) circular needle, 32in (80cm) long

Stitch marker

Tapestry needle

finished measurements
51in (129cm) circumference x 12in (30cm) wide

gauge (tension)
14 sts x 22 rows to measure 4in (10cm) over stockinette (stocking) stitch on US 10 (6mm) needles after blocking

abbreviations
See page 126.

tip Ensure you use a stitch marker to indicate the beginning of the round—it's easy to lose track of the start and end without one.

for the cowl

Using US 10 (6mm) needles and the moebius technique (see pages 114–115), cast on 180 sts. Place a stitch marker to indicate beginning of the round.

Rounds 1–4: Knit.
Rounds 5–10: K1, *k2tog, yo; rep from * to last st, k1.
Rounds 11–14: Purl.
Rounds 15–20: K1, *k2tog, yo; rep from * to last st, k1.
Rounds 21–24: Knit.
Round 25: K1, *k2tog, yo; rep from * to last st, k1.
Round 26: Purl.
Round 27: [K1, p1] to end.
Bind (cast) off knitwise.

making up and finishing

Weave in all loose ends and block to measurements.

tip Each round is worked by knitting the upper stitches then flowing directly into the second lower set of stitches and you won't even realize a twist is being created! You have completed one full round when the stitch marker appears between the needles again and you can slip it from one to the next.

make it yours Once you get the hang of the moebius technique play with variegated yarns, different colors, shades, and textures to create a completely different look. These cowls make great gifts and are easy to personalize.

chapter 2

warm
and rich

tips

The stitch marker acts as a reminder to work the three bottom-edge stitches in stockinette (stocking) stitch, to give a neat rolled finish to the shawl.

To ensure you have enough yarn, divide the fifth ball into 2 balls of equal weight; if you use 2½ balls before you finish the Increase section, you may need to reduce the size of the shawl or change your gauge (tension).

spice rack

This simple shawl is worked from one side to the other in garter stitch, and is the perfect mid-season cover up. Accent the points with over-sized tassels for a stylish finish.

materials

Lion Brand Vanna's Choice (100% acrylic, approx 170yd/156m per 3½oz/100g ball) worsted (Aran) weight yarn
  5 balls of shade Rose 142 (A)
  Small amount (less than 1 ball) of shade Mustard 158 (B)

US 10 (6mm) circular needle, 40in (100cm) length

Note: The shawl is worked flat in rows but a circular needle is recommended due to the high stitch count.

Stitch marker

Tapestry needle

finished measurements

79in (200cm) wide x 35in (89cm) deep

gauge (tension)

14 sts x 24 rows to measure 4in (10cm) over garter stitch on US 10 (6mm) needles after blocking

abbreviations

See page 126

special abbreviations

pm place marker
sm slip marker

make it yours Add a second shade and create vertical stripes by alternating yarn colors every few rows.

tip Take time to tie the strands of the tassels together securely using a double knot after fastening them to the points of the shawl.

for the shawl

Increase section

Using US 10 (6mm) needles and yarn A, cast on 3 sts.
Row 1 (RS): Knit to end.
Row 2 (WS): K1, kfb, k1. *4 sts*
Row 3: K2, pm, kfb, k1. *5 sts*
Row 4: K to last 3 sts, p1, sm, p2.
Row 5: K2, sm, kfb, k to end. *1 st inc*
Rows 6–241: Rep rows 4 and 5. *124 sts*

Decrease section

Row 242 (WS): K to last 3 sts, p1, sm, p2.
Row 243 (RS): K2, sm, k2tog, k to end. *1 st dec*
Rep rows 242–243 until 3 sts remain ending with a RS row.
Next row: Knit.
Bind (cast) off knitwise.

making up and finishing

Weave in all loose ends and block to measurements.

for the tassels

Make 3 alike

For each tassel, braid 3 x 4in (10cm) lengths of yarn B together and knot to secure.

Feed a braid through each point of shawl and secure to create a loop.

Cut 24 x 16in (40cm) lengths of yarn B and feed through braided loop.

Fold the strands in half and tie a 4in (10cm) length of yarn B around the strands to secure.

Trim ends to neaten.

falling leaves

This compact neck warmer features a clever gap to feed one end of the shawl through, to hold it snugly in place. Because it's worked from the bottom, pointed section upward, you can increase the size simply by knitting more rows, until your yarn runs out!

materials

Brown Sheep Company Lamb's Pride Worsted (85% wool, 15% mohair, approx 190yd/173m per 4oz/113g ball) worsted (Aran) weight yarn

2 balls of shade Autumn Harvest M22 (A)

Small amount (less than 1 ball) of shade Sandy Heather M01 (B)

US 8 (5mm) circular needle, 40in (100cm) length

Note: The shawl is worked flat in rows but a circular needle is recommended due to the high stitch count.

US H/8 (5mm) crochet hook

Tapestry needle

finished measurements

43in (110cm) wide x 21in (53cm) deep

gauge (tension)

16 sts x 33 rows to measure 4in (10cm) over garter stitch on US 8 (5mm) needles after blocking

abbreviations

See page 126.

pattern note

The border is worked in crochet. US and UK crochet terms differ and the same term is used for different stitches. Both versions have been given here.

make it yours Increase the contrast by working the crochet border and the keyhole opening in two different shades.

for the neck warmer

Using US 8 (5mm) needle and yarn A, cast on 2 sts.
Row 1: Knit.
Row 2: K1, kfb. *3 sts*
Row 3: K1, kfb, k to end. *1 st inc*
Rows 4–149: Rep row 3. *150 sts*
Row 150 (Keyhole): K1, kfb, k to last 40 sts, bind (cast) off next 20 sts, k to end.
Row 151: K1, kfb, k18, using the backward loop method (see page 113), cast on 20 sts, k to end. *152 sts*
Rows 152–170: Rep row 3. *171 sts*
Bind (cast) off knitwise.

making up and finishing

Weave in all loose ends and block to measurements.

for the crochet border

Using US H/8 (5mm) crochet hook, join yarn B in any row end, work 1ch then 1sc (UK: 1dc) in each stitch and row end around the shawl, working 2sc (UK: 2dc) in each corner and joining the round with a sl st in the first sc (UK: dc). Fasten off and repeat for the keyhole opening.

Weave in any remaining ends.

tips Double check the sizing of the neck warmer by slipping it on as you go. If necessary, increase the size by knitting more rows, increasing as set in the pattern and remember that increasing the size will require additional yarn.

If you don't crochet, simply work a row of blanket stitch in a contrast yarn around the edges of the neck warmer and the keyhole opening.

tip This design is worked in the round, which means that knitting all the stitches will result in a stockinette (stocking) stitch fabric.

midnight sky

Worked in a twisted loop, this cozy wrap will stay snug around your shoulders without the need for fiddly fasteners. Select three toning shades for an ombré design, or pick clashing brights for a bolder statement.

materials

Brown Sheep Company Lamb's Pride Worsted (85% wool, 15% mohair, approx 190yd/173m per 4oz/113g ball) worsted (Aran) weight yarn

2 balls each of shades:
Blue Flannel M82 (A)
Sapphire M65 (B)
Periwinkle M59 (C)

US 10 (6mm) circular needle, 32–40in (80–100cm) length

Stitch marker

Tapestry needle

finished measurements

43in (109cm) circumference x 26in (66cm) deep

gauge (tension)

15 sts x 25 rows to measure 4in (10cm) over stockinette (stocking) stitch on US 10 (6mm) needles after blocking.

abbreviations

See page 126.

for the wrap

Using US 10 (6mm) circular needle and yarn A, cast on 160 sts.

Create a single twist in the stitches by moving the RH needle one turn counter-(anti-) clockwise and join for working in the round, placing a stitch marker to indicate beginning of round.

Knit every round until piece measures 12in (30cm) from cast-on edge.

Fasten off yarn A, leaving a tail to weave in, and join yarn B.

Knit every round until piece measures 19in (48cm) from cast-on edge.

Fasten off yarn B leaving a tail to weave in and join yarn C.

Knit every round until piece measures 26in (66cm) from cast-on edge.

Bind (cast) off knitwise taking care not to work too tightly.

making up and finishing

Weave in all loose ends and block to measurements.

make it yours This wrap is designed to sit snugly around your shoulders. You can customize the fit by simply increasing or decreasing the number of stitches cast on.

patchwork patterns

Mitered squares are quick to make and a perfect on-the-go project! When joined together they become a fantastic modular design.

materials

Cascade 220 (100% Peruvian highland wool, approx 220yd/200m per 3½oz/100g skein) worsted (Aran) weight yarn

   1 skein each of shades

   Natural 8010 (A)

   Dusty Rose 8114 (B)

   Orchid Mist 9631 (C)

   Regal 7807 (D)

   Lily Pad 9637 (E)

   Vermeer Blue 9419 (F)

US 8 (5mm) knitting needles

1 stitch marker

Tapestry needle

finished measurements

20in (51cm) wide x 56in (142cm) long

gauge (tension)

Each mitered square to measure 4¾ x 4¾in (12 x 12cm) after blocking

abbreviations

See page 126.

make it yours Mitered squares are great for using up leftover yarn from your stash as each square can be made in a different shade or style of yarn for a really eclectic finish! Just remember to work with yarns of a similar weight and gauge (tension) to ensure that each block is the same size.

F	C	E	D	A	14
B	F	C	E	D	13
A	B	F	C	E	12
D	A	B	F	C	11
E	D	A	B	F	10
C	E	D	A	B	9
F	C	E	D	A	8
B	F	C	E	D	7
A	B	F	C	E	6
D	A	B	F	C	5
E	D	A	B	F	4
C	E	D	A	B	3
F	C	E	D	A	2
B	F	C	E	D	1

for each miter square

Using US 8 (5mm) needles and your shade of choice, cast on 36 sts and pm between sts 18 and 19.

Row 1 (RS): K to 2 sts before marker, ssk, sm, k2tog, k to end. *2 sts dec*

Row 2 (WS): Knit.

Rep rows 1–2 until only 2 sts remain, removing marker when no longer needed.

Next row: K2tog. Break yarn leaving a 4in (10cm) tail and pull through the remaining st to fasten off.

Weave in ends and block each square to measurements.

for the wrap

Make 11 squares in each yarn A and B. Make 12 squares in each yarn C, D, E, and F.

making up and finishing

Lay the squares into 14 rows of 5 squares in the following order (see chart, above):

Row 1: B, F, C, E, D
Row 2: F, C, E, D, A
Row 3: C, E, D, A, B
Row 4: E, D, A, B, F
Row 5: D, A, B, F, C
Row 6: A, B, F, C, E
Row 7: B, F, C, E, D
Row 8: F, C, E, D, A
Row 9: C, E, D, A, B
Row 10: E, D, A, B, F
Row 11: D, A, B, F, C
Row 12: A, B, F, C, E
Row 13: B, F, C, E, D
Row 14: F, C, E, D, A

Join the squares into rows with mattress, stitch (see page 124), then join the rows together.

Weave in any remaining ends and block to measurements.

tip Two decreases are used in this pattern; ssk, which leans to the left and k2tog, which leans to the right. Worked in combination, these form a neat point toward the center.

tip Use a stitch marker to indicate the center point of the row to help you keep track of your place in the pattern and maintain correct placement of the decreases.

draped cape

Drape this luxurious and cozy crescent-shaped shawl around your shoulders to beat the chills.

materials

Cascade Melilla (45% silk, 35% wool, 20% nylon, approx 220yd/200m per 3½oz/100g ball) worsted (Aran) weight yarn
  4 balls of shade Flora 02

US 9 (5.5mm) circular needle, minimum 40in (100cm) length

Note: The wrap is worked flat in rows but a circular needle is recommended due to the high stitch count.

2 stitch markers

Tapestry needle

finished measurements

59in (150cm) wide along top edge x 27½in (70cm) deep

gauge (tension)

16 sts x 24 rows to measure 4in (10cm) over stockinette (stocking) stitch on US 9 (5.5mm) needles

abbreviations

See page 126.

tip Use a decorative pin to secure the shawl around your shoulder or add a button and loop if preferred.

for the shawl

Garter tab cast on

Using US 9 (5.5mm) needles, cast on 4 sts.

Knit 10 rows but **do not** turn on the last row.

Pick up and k4 sts in the long edge (1 st in each garter ridge), then pick up and k4 sts along the cast-on edge. *12 sts*

Knit 1 row.

Garter yoke

Row 1 (RS): K4, pm, kfb in each st to last 4 sts, pm, k4. *16 sts; 2 markers placed—slip these as you pass them on all subsequent rows*

Rows 2–4: Knit.

Row 5: K to marker, sm, kfb in each st to marker, sm, k to end. *24 sts*

Rows 6–10: Knit.

Row 11: K to marker, sm, kfb in each st to marker, sm, k to end. *40 sts*

Rows 12–22: Knit.

Row 23: K to marker, sm, kfb in each st to marker, sm, k to end. *72 sts*

Rows 24–46: Knit.

Stockinette (stocking) stitch body

Row 47 (RS): K to marker, sm, [yo, k1] to marker, yo, sm, k to end. *137 sts*

Row 48 (WS): K4, sm, p to last marker, sm, k4.

Row 49: Knit.

Row 50: K4, sm, p to last marker, sm, k4.

Rows 51–94: Rep rows 49–50.

Row 95: K to marker, sm, [yo, k1] to marker, sm, k to end. *266 sts*

Row 96: K4, sm, p to last marker, sm, k4.

Row 97: Knit.

Rows 98–143: Rep rows 96–97.

Ribbed border

Row 144 (WS): [K2, p2] to last 2 sts, k2.

Row 145 (RS): [P2, k2] to last 2 sts, p2.

Rows 146–163: Rep rows 144–145.

Bind (cast) off in rib pattern.

making up and finishing

Weave in all loose ends and block to measurements.

tip This shawl uses a system called the Pi method which increases in a gradual sequence to create the curved shape.

make it yours I made this shawl in a single variegated yarn, but you could use a different color for each of the three different elements—garter stitch yoke, stockinette (stocking) stitch body, and ribbed border.

madeira wine

A single row lace pattern makes this rectangular wrap not only deceptively simple to knit, but quick and easy to master as well, so before you know it you'll be cozied up in a light and airy accessory!

materials

Rowan Kidsilk Haze (70% mohair, 20% silk, approx 229yd/210m per 1oz/25g ball) 2ply (lace) weight yarn
  2 balls of shade Liqueur 595

US 8 (5mm) knitting needles

Tapestry needle

finished measurements

16in (40cm) wide x 63in (160cm) long

gauge (tension)

16 sts x 20 rows to measure 4in (10cm) over lace pattern on US 8 (5mm) needles after blocking

abbreviations

See page 126.

make it yours Create an ombré wrap by picking three yarns in different tones of the same color and work from light to dark, or use leftovers from your stash for a multi-colored, striped shawl.

for the wrap

Using US 8 (5mm) needles, loosely cast on 64 sts.
Knit 2 rows.
Lace row: *K1, yo, p2tog, k1; rep from * to end.
Rep Lace row until work measures 62in (155cm) from cast-on edge, or to desired length.

Knit 2 rows.
Bind (cast) off loosely knitwise.

making up and finishing

Weave in all loose ends and block to measurements, opening up the lace.

tip Owing to the long mohair fibers, this yarn can be very tricky to unravel if you make mistakes, so keep checking your work and stitch counts as you go to avoid or identify any mistakes quickly.

tip Ensure you cast on and bind (cast) off loosely so the top and bottom edges stretch to the same width as the main fabric. Using a slightly larger needle than the gauge (tension) knitting needle will help to keep the stitches loose.

moonlight and lace

This pretty crescent shawl teams classic knitted fabric with a delicate lace panel to give it a lovely feminine finish.

materials

Fyberspates Gleem Lace (55% wool, 45% silk, approx 874yd/800m per 3½oz/100g skein) 2ply (lace) weight yarn
  1 ball of shade Tweed Imps 701

US 6 (4mm) circular needle, minimum 40in (100cm) length

Note: The shawl is worked flat in rows but a circular needle is recommended due to the high stitch count.

US 8 (5mm) knitting needle for bind (cast) off

2 stitch markers

Tapestry Needle

finished measurements

47in (120cm) wide along top edge x 18in (45cm) deep

gauge (tension)

28 sts x 32 rows to measure 4in (10cm) over stockinette (stocking) stitch on US 6 (4mm) needles after blocking

abbreviations

See page 126.

tip This pattern uses a stretchy bind (cast) off method, which is worked by knitting stitches and passing them back to the left-hand needle before binding (casting) them off, thus creating extra length in the edge so you can fully block out the shawl into a neat crescent shape.

make it yours This design can also be worked in a light worsted (DK) or worsted (Aran) weight yarn for a heavier finish. Be sure to adjust the yarn amounts accordingly.

for the shawl

Garter tab cast on
Using US 6 (4mm) needles, cast on 3 sts.
Knit 6 rows but **do not** turn on the last row.
Pick up and k3 sts in the long edge (1 st in each garter ridge), then pick up and k3 sts along the cast-on edge. *9 sts*
Knit 1 row.

Stockinette (stocking) stitch section
Row 1 (RS): K3, pm, yo, [k1, yo] 3 times, pm, k3. *13 sts; 2 markers placed—slip these as you pass them on all subsequent rows*
Row 2 (WS): K3, p to last 3 sts, k3.
Row 3: K3, sm, yo, k7, yo, sm, k3. *15 sts*
Row 4: K3, p to last 3 sts, k3.
Row 5: K3, sm, yo, [k1, yo] 9 times, sm, k3. *25 sts*
Row 6: K3, p to last 3 sts, k3.
Row 7: K3, sm, yo, k to last 3 sts, yo, sm, k3. *2 sts inc*
Row 8: K3, p to last 3 sts, k3.
Rows 9–20: Rep rows 7–8. *39 sts*
Row 21: K3, sm, yo, [k1, kfb] 15 times, k3, yo, sm, k3. *56 sts*
Row 22: K3, p to last 3 sts, k3.
Rows 23–32: Rep rows 7–8. *66 sts*
Row 33: K3, sm, yo [k2, kfb] 19 times, k3, yo, sm, k3. *87 sts*
Row 34: K3, p to last 3 sts, k3.
Rows 35–44: Rep rows 7–8. *97 sts*
Row 45: K3, sm, yo, [k3, kfb] 22 times, k3, yo, sm, k3. *121 sts*
Row 46: K3, p to last 3 sts, k3.
Rows 47–56: Rep rows 7–8. *131 sts*
Row 57: K3, sm, yo, [k4, kfb] 24 times, k5, yo, sm, k3. *157 sts*
Row 58: K3, p to last 3 sts, k3.
Rows 59–68: Rep rows 7–8. *167 sts*
Row 69: K3, sm, yo, [k5, kfb] 26 times, k5, yo, sm, k3. *195 sts*
Row 70: K3, p to last 3 sts, k3.
Rows 71–80: Rep rows 7–8. *205 sts*
Row 81: K3, sm, yo, [k7, kfb] 24 times, k7, yo, sm, k3. *231 sts*
Row 82: K3, p to last 3 sts, k3.

tip When working the lace section, you may find it useful to place a stitch marker after every 10-stitch repeat to help keep you on track.

Rows 83–92: Rep rows 7–8. *241 sts*
Row 93: K3, sm, yo, k6, [k8, kfb] 24 times, k13, yo, sm, k3. *267 sts*
Row 94: K3, p to last 3 sts, k3.

Lace panel section
Row 1 (RS): K4, *yo, k3, sl1 k2tog psso, k3, yo, k1; rep from * to last 3 sts, k3.
Row 2 (WS): K3, p to last 3 sts, k3.
Row 3: K4, *k1, yo, k2, sl1 k2tog psso, k2, yo, k2; rep from * to last 3 sts, k3.
Row 4: K3, p to last 3 sts, k3.
Row 5: K4, *k2, yo, k1, sl1 k2tog psso, k1, yo, k3; rep from * to last 3 sts, k3.
Row 6: K3, p to last 3 sts, k3.
Row 7: K4, *k3, yo, sl1 k2tog psso, yo, k4; rep from * to last 3 sts, k3.
Row 8: K3, p to last 3 sts, k3.
Rep Lace Panel rows 1–8 a further 5 times.

Stretchy bind (cast) off
Using US 8 (5mm) needles, k2, *slip sts back to LH needle without twisting, k2tog tbl, k1; rep from * to end.
Break yarn and pull through remaining st to fasten off.

making up and finishing
Weave in all loose ends and block firmly to measurements, opening the lace pattern and shaping the shawl into a crescent.

a splash of orange

This elegant, airy wrap is worked in two contrasting shades of 2ply (lace) weight yarn to create a modern color pop accessory. The rectangular shape and simple pattern makes this an ideal project for getting accustomed to working with fine yarns.

materials

Debbie Bliss Rialto Lace (100% Merino wool, approx 427yd/390m per 1¾oz/50g ball) 2ply (lace) weight yarn
   2 balls of shade Medium Grey 003 (A)
   1 ball of shade Coral 026 (B)

US 8 (5mm) knitting needles

Tapestry needle

finished measurements

15½in (40cm) wide x 48in (120cm) long

gauge (tension)

20 sts x 24 rows to measure 4in (10cm) over stockinette (stocking) stitch on US 8 (5mm) needles

abbreviations

See page 126.

for the neck wrap

Using US 8 (5mm) needles and yarn A, loosely cast on 70 sts.
Row 1 (RS): [K10, p10] 3 times, k10.
Row 2 (WS): [P10, k10] 3 times, p10.
Rep rows 1–2 until piece measures 48in (120cm) from cast-on edge.
Bind (cast) off loosely knitwise.

for the contrast stripe

With RS facing, using the US 8 (5mm) needle and yarn B, pick up and k1 st in each row end along one long edge of piece—exact stitch count isn't crucial.
Knit 14 rows.
Bind (cast) off loosely knitwise.

making up and finishing

Weave in all loose ends and block to measurements.

tips If you find the yarn too slippery to work with when using metal needles, change over to a wooden or bamboo set, which will provide more grip for the fiber.

Lightweight yarns can easily get in a tangle—try stowing your project in a knitting bag or ziplock bag to keep the yarn ball tidy as you work.

make it yours For extra "pop," add a third contrasting shade of yarn, switching halfway through the yarn B section.

raspberry and rhubarb

As the evenings begin to turn chilly, this lightweight cowl will make the perfect, handy addition to your fall wardrobe. The knitted lace stitch works up to create an elegant overlapping waves pattern, before being blocked and seamed to create a neat lace cowl.

materials
Malabrigo Lace (100% Merino wool, approx 470yd/430m per 1¾oz/50g skein) 2ply (lace) weight yarn
  1 skein of shade Col China 001

US 4 (3.5mm) knitting needles

Tapestry needle

finished measurements
26in (66cm) circumference x 10in (26cm) deep

gauge (tension)
25 sts x 32 rows to measure 4in (10cm) over lace pattern on US 4 (3.5mm) needles after blocking

abbreviations
See page 126.

tip The delicate yarn used in the cowl is purchased as a skein. Take time to wind it gently into a ball by hand before you start, to prevent any nasty tangles as you knit.

tip If you are new to lace knitting you might find it helpful to place a stitch marker after the first two stitches, then markers after every six-stitch repeat across the row. You will need 11 stitch markers in total and simply slip them from needle to needle as you knit.

make it yours This cowl is easy to resize; to make it deeper, cast on more stitches in a multiple of 6 plus 4 and adjust the circumference by working to a longer length before binding (casting) off and seaming together. Remember to allow extra yarn for any changes.

for the cowl

Using US 4 (3.5mm) needles, cast on 64 sts.

Row 1 (RS): K2, *yo, ssk, k4; rep from * to last 2 sts, yo, k2tog.

Row 2 (WS): Purl.

Row 3: K2, *yo, k1, ssk, k3; rep from * to last 2 sts, yo, k2tog.

Row 4: Purl.

Row 5: K2, *yo, k2, ssk, k2; rep from * to last 2 sts, yo, k2tog.

Row 6: Purl.

Row 7: K2, *yo, k3, ssk, k1; rep from * to last 2 sts, yo, k2tog.

Row 8: Purl.

Row 9: K2, *yo, k4, ssk; rep from * to last 2 sts, yo, k2tog.

Row 10: Purl.

Rep rows 1–10 until piece measures 25in (63cm) from cast-on edge ending with a WS row.

Bind (cast) off loosely knitwise.

making up and finishing

Weave in all loose ends and block to measurements, opening up the lace pattern.

Align the two shorter ends and join with mattress stitch (see page 124).

golden sunshine

This long and chunky wrap features a small textured panel through which one end can be passed, allowing you to secure it snugly around yourself.

materials

Lion Brand Hometown USA (100% acrylic, approx 81yd/74m per 5oz/142g ball) super-bulky (super-chunky) yarn
   4 balls of shade Las Vegas Gold 170 (A)
   1 ball of shade Dallas Grey 149 (B)

US 13 (9mm) knitting needles

US M/13 (9mm) crochet hook

Tapestry needle

finished measurements

16in (40cm) wide x 71in (180cm) long

gauge (tension)

8 sts x 12 rows to measure 4in (10cm) over stockinette (stocking) stitch on US 13 (9mm) needles after blocking

abbreviations

See page 126.

make it yours This wrap is worked in a super-bulky (super-chunky) yarn, however you could make a lightweight version by switching to a finer yarn. Bear in mind that this will also make it smaller but the pattern can easily be resized by casting on a multiple of 5 stitches plus 3 and adjusting the size of the seed (moss) stitch fastening panel as required.

tip Slip the wrap on before securing the seed (moss) stitch fastening panel in place to be sure that you are happy with the placement.

for the shawl

Using US 13 (9mm) needles and yarn A, cast on 33 sts.

Row 1 (RS): *K3, p2; rep from * to last 3 sts, k3.

Row 2 (WS): *P3, k2, rep from * to last 3 sts, p3.

Rep rows 1–2 until piece measures 69in (175cm) from cast-on edge.

Bind (cast) off in pattern.

Fastening panel

Using US 13 (9mm) needles and yarn B, cast on 11 sts.

Row 1: *K1, p1; rep from * to last st, k1.

Last row sets seed (moss) stitch.

Rep row 1 until piece measures 9in (22.5cm) from cast-on edge.

Bind (cast) off in pattern.

Place the fastening panel onto the wrap approx 16in (40cm) up from the wrap cast-on edge, aligning it neatly with the ribbed pattern. Secure in place with mattress stitch (see page 124) along the two short edges of the panel.

Crochet border

Using US 13 (9mm) hook, join yarn B in any row end. Work 1ch then 1sc (UK: 1dc) in each st and row end around the shawl, working 2sc (UK: 2dc) in each corner and joining the round with a sl st in first sc (UK: dc).

Fasten off.

making up and finishing

Weave in all loose ends and block to measurements.

tip If you prefer not to crochet the border, embroider blanket stitch around the outer edge instead.

rosy red wrap

This luxurious, rectangular wrap is worked in a delicate yarn incorporating a leaf motif pattern for an elegant summery look. As the lace stitch repeat is worked on both right and wrong side rows, this make is more suited to advanced knitters familiar with lace knitting patterns.

materials
Fyberspates Scrumptious Lace (55% Merino wool, 45% silk, approx 1093yd/1000m per 3½oz/100g skein) 2ply (lace) weight yarn
   1 skein of shade Rose Pink 509

US 6 (4mm) knitting needles

Tapestry needle

finished measurements
19in (48cm) wide x 48in (120cm)

gauge (tension)
20 sts x 24 rows to measure 4in (10cm) over lace pattern on US 6 (4mm) needles after firm blocking

abbreviations
See page 126.

make it yours For additional sparkle and drape, knit small beads into the design as you work.

for the wrap

Using US 6 (4mm) needles, loosely cast on 99 sts.

Bottom border
Rows 1–5: Knit.

Lace pattern
Row 1 (RS): K4, *k1, yo, k1, ssk, p1, k2tog, k1, yo, p1, ssk, p1, k2tog, yo, k1, yo; rep from * to last 5 sts, k5.

Row 2 (WS): K4, p1, *p4, k1, p1, k1, p3, k1, p4; rep from * to last 4 sts, k4.

Row 3: K4, *k1, yo, k1, ssk, p1, k2tog, k1, p1, sl1, k2tog, psso, yo, k3, yo; rep from * to last 5 sts, k5. *93 sts*

Row 4: K4, p1, *p6, k1, p2, k1, p4; rep from * to last 4 sts, k4.

Row 5: K4, *[k1, yo] twice, ssk, p1, [k2tog] twice, yo, k5, yo; rep from * to last 5 sts, k5. *99 sts*

Row 6: K4, p1, *p7, k1, p1, k1, p5; rep from * to last 4 sts, k4.

Row 7: K4, *k1, yo, k3, yo, sl1 k2tog psso, p1, yo, k1, ssk, p1, k2tog, k1, yo; rep from * to last 5 sts, k5.

Row 8: K4, p1, *[p3, k1] twice, p7; rep from *to last 4 sts, k4.

Row 9: K4, *k1, yo, k5, yo, ssk, k1, ssk, p1, k2tog, k1, yo; rep from * to last 5 sts, k5.

Row 10: K4, p1, *p3, k1, p2, k1, p8; rep from * to last 4 sts, k4.

Rep lace rows 1–10 a further 27 times.

Top border
Rows 1–5: Knit.
Bind (cast) off loosely.

making up and finishing

Weave in all loose ends and block firmly to measurements, opening up the lace pattern.

tips Insert a lifeline by running a smooth, thin length of cotton yarn after each 10-row lace repeat to catch the stitches should you need to rip back your work (see page 8).

Silk blend yarns can be slippery to work with. Try using bamboo or wooden needles to help "grip" the stitches.

chapter 3

natural
and neutral

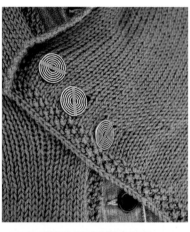

make it yours For even greater contrast, use opposite rather than complementary colors.

waves and water

Working with yarns made of different fibers can create wonderful effects and textured finishes. This shawl, knitted from the tip upward, plays with the contrast between two yarns to great effect.

materials
Katia Big Ribbon (50% cotton, 50% polyester, approx 78yd/72m per 7oz/200g ball) super-bulky (super-chunky) weight yarn
   1 ball of shade 022 (A)

Debbie Bliss Paloma (60% baby alpaca, 40% merino wool, approx 71yd/65m per 1¾oz/50g ball) super-bulky (super-chunky) weight yarn
   6 balls of shade Jade 028 (B)

US 17 (12mm) circular needle, 48in (120cm) length

Note: The shawl is worked flat in rows but a circular needle is recommended due to the high stitch count.

Tapestry needle

finished measurements
80½in (205cm) along upper edge x 37½in (95cm) deep at widest point

gauge (tension)
8 sts x 13 rows to measure 4in (10cm) over garter stitch on US 17 (12mm) needles after blocking and using yarn B

abbreviations
See page 126.

for the shawl
Using US 17 (12mm) needles and yarn A, cast on 3 sts.
Row 1: K1, kfb, k to end. *1 st inc*
Rows 2–49: Rep row 1. *52 sts*
Break yarn A leaving a tail to weave in.
Row 50 (Eyelets): Using yarn B, k2, *k2tog, yo; rep from * to last 2 sts, k2.
Row 51: Knit.
Rows 52–99: Rep row 1. *100 sts*
Row 100: K1, kfb, k to last 2 sts, kfb, k1. *2 sts inc*
Rows 101–132: Rep row 100. *166 sts*
Bind (cast) off knitwise.

making up and finishing
Weave in all loose ends and block to measurements taking time to open out the eyelets in row 50.

tips A row of eyelets is created halfway up the shawl by working an increase (yo) paired with a decrease (k2tog). This does not alter the stitch count.

The different structures and weights of yarn used in this project make the lower portion heavier. Secure your shawl with a pin or with a brooch to keep it in position during wear.

sea green

Worked in a multi-tonal yarn, this tactile shawl contrasts different stitch patterns for a textured and cozy finish.

materials

Berroco Comfort (50% super fine nylon, 50% super fine acrylic, approx 210yd/190m per 3½oz/100g ball) worsted (Aran) weight yarn
   3 balls of shade Galaxy Mix 9808

US 9 (5.5mm) circular needle, minimum 40in (100cm) length

Note: The shawl is worked flat in rows but a circular needle is recommended due to the high stitch count.

2 stitch markers

Tapestry needle

finished measurements

58in (148cm) wide x 29in (74cm) deep

gauge (tension)

16 sts x 22 rows to measure 4in (10cm) over stockinette (stocking) stitch on US 9 (5.5mm) needles after blocking

abbreviations

See page 126.

special abbreviations

pm place marker
sm slip marker

make it yours This design is worked in a variegated yarn, but for additional impact you could use a solid color for the stockinette (stocking) stitch section and contrast it with a variegated yarn for the seed (moss) stitch rows.

for the shawl

Using US 9 (5.5mm) needles, cast on 5 sts.

Set-up row 1 (RS): K1, yo, k1, yo, pm, k1, pm, yo, k1, yo, k1. 9 sts; *2 markers placed—slip these as you pass them on all subsequent rows*

Set-up row 2 (WS): Purl.

Stockinette (stocking) stitch section

Row 1 (RS): K2, yo, k to marker, yo, sm, k1, sm, yo, k to last 2 sts, yo, k2. *4 sts inc*

Row 2 (WS): Purl.

Rows 3–24: Rep rows 1–2. *57 sts*

Seed (moss) stitch section

Row 25 (RS): K2, yo, [k1, p1] to marker, yo, sm, k1, sm, yo, [p1, k1] to last 2 sts, yo, k2. *4 sts inc*

Row 26 (WS): P2, [p1, k1] to marker, sm, p1, sm, [k1, p1] to last 2 sts, p2.

Row 27 (RS): K2, yo, [p1, k1] to marker, yo, sm, k1, sm, yo, [k1, p1] to last 2 sts, yo, k2. *4 sts inc*

Row 28 (WS): P2, [k1, p1] to marker, sm, k1, sm, [p1, k1] to last 2 sts, p2.

Rows 29–102: Rep rows 25–28. *213 sts*

Ribbed border

Row 103: K2, yo, [k4, p4] to marker, yo, sm, k1, sm, yo, [p4, k4] to last 2 sts, yo, k2. *4 sts inc*

Row 104: P2, k1, [p4, k4] to 1 st before marker, p1, sm, p1, sm, p1, [k4, p4] to last 3 sts, k1, p2.

Rows 103–104 set 4x4 rib pattern.

Rows 105–118: Continue in 4x4 rib for a further 14 rows, maintaining edge sts and center st in stockinette (stocking) stitch and taking the increased sts into 4x4 rib pattern, ending with a WS row. *245 sts*

Bind (cast) off knitwise.

making up and finishing

Weave in all loose ends and block to measurements.

---

tip Take care to ensure the yarn over increases (yo) either side of the central spine don't slip under the stitch markers. You should only ever have one stitch in between these two markers.

tip When working in seed (moss) stitch, you can keep your place by looking at the row below and determining which stitch you are on; stitches that were knitted on the previous row should be knitted, and vice versa.

skill level

pure and simple

This simple stitch is commonly used on dishcloths, but the distinctive texture and honeycomb motif make it a wonderful and unusual stitch pattern for accessories.

materials

Lion Brand Wool-Ease (80% acrylic, 20% wool, 197yd/180m per 3oz/85g ball) worsted (Aran) weight yarn
  4 balls of shade Fisherman 99

US 8 (5mm) knitting needles

Tapestry needle

finished measurements

17in (43cm) x 66in (168cm) long

gauge (tension)

16 sts x 26 rows to measure 4in (10cm) over slip stitch pattern on US 8 (5mm) needles after blocking.

abbreviations

See page 126.

make it yours Add tassels or fringing to the short ends for additional detail or work in four shades of yarn, alternating every eight rows for a striped look.

neutral and natural

tips Slip stitch patterns create a denser and cozier fabric than regular stockinette (stocking) stitch due to a higher concentration of rows within a set area.

Slip all the slip stitches purlwise with yarn in back.

for the shawl

Using US 8 (5mm) needles, cast on 69 sts.
Rows 1–4: Knit.
Row 5 (RS): Knit.
Row 6 (WS): K5, [sl1, k1] to last 4 sts, k4.
Row 7: Knit.
Row 8: K6, [sl1, k1] to last 5 sts, k5.
Rows 5–8 set the slip stitch pattern.
Rep rows 5–8 until piece measures approx 65in (166cm) from cast-on edge.
Knit 4 rows.
Bind (cast) off knitwise.

making up and finishing

Weave in all loose ends and block to measurements.

skill level

waves of warmth

A stunning variegated yarn brings out the details in the deceptively simple and fun stitch pattern used for this generous wrap.

materials

Malabrigo Worsted (100% wool, approx 209yd/192m per 3½oz/100g ball) worsted (Aran) weight yarn

   4 balls of shade Milonga 627

US 10 (6mm) knitting needles

Tapestry needle

finished measurements

25½in (65cm) wide x 55in (140cm) long

gauge (tension)

14 sts x 16 rows to measure 4in (10cm) over wave stitch on US 10 (6mm) needles after blocking.

abbreviations

See page 126.

make it yours Why not add oversized tassels to the corners of the wrap in a contrasting color!

for the wrap

Using US 10 (6mm) needles, cast on 86 sts.
Row 1 (RS): Knit.
Row 2 (WS): Knit.
Row 3: K6, *yo twice, k1, yo 3 times, k1, yo 4 times, k1, yo 3 times, k1, yo twice, k6; rep from * to end of row.
Row 4: Knit to end, dropping the yos as you go and allowing the knit sts between them to lengthen.
Row 5: Knit.
Row 6: Knit.
Row 7: K1, *yo twice, k1, yo 3 times, k1, yo 4 times, k1, yo 3 times, k1, yo twice, k6; rep from * to end of row, ending with k1 instead of k6.
Row 8: Knit to end, dropping the yos as you go and allowing the knit sts between them to lengthen.
Rep rows 1–8 a further 27 times.
Knit 2 rows.
Bind (cast) off.

making up and finishing

Weave in all loose ends and block to measurements.

tip The wavy look of this wrap is created with multiple yarn overs (yos). In a regular yarn over (yo) you take the yarn over the needle once, but for the wave pattern it is taken over two, three, or four times to create elongated stitches of varying lengths. It might take a few rows to get the hang of it but once you do you'll be flying along!

tip To keep track of where you are in a row, use stitch markers to denote the 10-stitch pattern repeats.

ice queen

Stay cozy with an ultra chunky knitted wrap! Worked in a thick and super squishy yarn on large needles, this rectangular wrap can be worked up in no time and is the perfect project for new knitters or last-minute knitted gifts.

materials

Lion Brand Wool-Ease Thick & Quick (80% acrylic, 20% wool, approx 106yd/97m per 6oz/170g ball) super-bulky (super-chunky) weight yarn
  7 balls of shade Glacier 105

US 15 (10mm) knitting needles

Tapestry needle

finished measurements

24in (60cm) wide x 86in (218cm) long

gauge (tension)

8 sts x 15 rows to measure 4in (10cm) over garter stitch on US 15 (10mm) needles after blocking

abbreviations

See page 126.

make it yours For a more distinctive finish, add colorful fringing to each end of the finished wrap.

for the wrap

Using US 15 (10mm) needles, cast on
50 sts.
Row 1: Knit.
Rep row 1 to create the garter stitch fabric
and continue until piece measures approx
86in (218cm) from cast-on edge or until
you have nearly used all the yarn, leaving
sufficient for the bind (cast) off—a length
of approx 3 times the width of the wrap
should be enough.
Bind (cast) off knitwise, taking care not to
work too tightly.

making up and finishing

Weave in all loose ends and block to
measurements.

tip Garter stitch looks the same on both
the front and the back, so there is no
"right side" on this wrap. Take care to
weave in all ends neatly to ensure they
are not visible on either side of the
finished piece.

tip Due to the volume of yarn, this wrap
can get pretty heavy! If you want to
increase the length consider reducing the
width slightly, so it doesn't become too
bulky to wear.

peppermint candy

This simple triangular shawl uses yarns of different weights for a really dramatic contrast; the combination of silky and fluffy yarns makes it great for evening wear!

materials
GGH Mystik (54% cotton, 46% rayon, approx 120yd/110m per 1¾oz/50g ball) light worsted (DK) weight yarn
  5 balls of shade Morgennebel 075 (A)

GGH Kid Melange (65% mohair, 30% nylon, 5% wool, approx 273yd/250m per 1oz/25g ball) 2ply (lace) weight yarn
  1 ball of shade Weiß 01 (B)

US 7 (4.5mm) circular needle, minimum 40in (100cm) length

Note: The wrap is worked flat in rows but a circular needle is recommended due to the high stitch count.

2 stitch markers

Tapestry needle

finished measurements
76in (193cm) wide x 35½in (90cm) deep

gauge (tension)
20 sts x 26 rows to measure 4in (10cm) over stockinette (stocking) stitch on US 7 (4.5mm) needles in yarn A after blocking

abbreviations
See page 126.

special abbreviations
pm place marker
sm slip marker

make it yours For a floatier finish to your shawl, work the yarns in the opposite order remembering to adjust the quantities accordingly.

for the shawl

Set-up
Using US 7 (4.5mm) needles and yarn A, cast on 7 sts.

Set up row 1 (RS): K2, yo, k1, yo, pm, k1, pm, yo, k1, yo, pm, k2. *11 sts; 2 markers placed—slip these as you pass them on all subsequent rows*

Set-up row 2 (WS): Purl.

Body of Shawl
Row 1 (RS): K2, sm, yo, k to marker, yo, sm, k1, sm, yo, k to last 2 sts, sm, k2. *4 sts inc*

Row 2 (WS): Purl.

Rows 3–100: Rep rows 1–2. *211 sts*

Rows 101–120: Change to yarn B and rep rows 1–2. *251 sts*

Rows 121–140: Change to yarn A and rep rows 1–2. *291 sts*

Rows 141–160: Change to yarn B and rep rows 1–2. *331 sts*

Rows 161–180: Change to yarn A and rep rows 1–2. *371 sts*

Row 181: K2, sm, yo, k to marker, yo, sm, k1, sm, yo, k to last 2 sts, sm, k2. *4 sts inc*

Row 182: Knit.

Rows 183–186: Rep rows 181–182. *383 sts*

Row 187: Rep row 181. *387 sts*
Bind (cast) off knitwise.

making up and finishing
Weave in all loose ends and block to measurements.

tip Different fibers are different to knit with. Changing the style of needle from metal to bamboo or wood can help grip the slippery mohair yarn and keep the stitches neat and even.

sun and sand

Worked from one side to the other, this triangular shawl incorporates a band of two-color brioche stitch as a dramatic focal point at the deepest part of the shawl.

materials

Brown Sheep Company Lamb's Pride Worsted (85% wool, 15% mohair, approx 189yd/173m per 4oz/113g ball) worsted (Aran) weight yarn

    2 balls of shade Sandy Heather M01 (A
    2 balls of shade Sunburst Gold M14 (B)

US 10 (6mm) circular needle, minimum 40in (100cm) length

Note: The shawl is worked flat in rows but a circular needle is recommended due to the high stitch count.

Stitch marker

Tapestry needle

finished measurements

69in (176cm) wide x 30in (76cm) deep

gauge (tension)

12 sts x 22 rows to measure 4in (10cm) over garter stitch on US 10 (6mm) needles relaxed after blocking

abbreviations

See page 126.

special brioche knitting abbreviations

k2tog: Knit the slipped stitch and yarn over next to it together

p2tog: Purl the slipped stitch and yarn over next to it together

sl1: Slip stitch purlwise with yarn held at back

sl1 wyif: Slip stitch purlwise with yarn held at front

yo: Take yarn over needle from front to back creating a yarn over

yof: Take yarn over needle from front to back and to the front again, creating a yarn over

for the shawl

Increase section

Using US 10 (6mm) needles and yarn A, cast on 3 sts.

Row 1 (RS): Knit.

Row 2 (WS): K1, kfb, k1. *4 sts*

Row 3: K2, pm, kfb, k1. *5 sts*

Row 4: Knit.

Row 5: K2, sm, kfb, k to end. *1 st inc*

Row 6: Knit.

Rows 7–174: Rep rows 5–6. *90 sts*

Rows 175–176: Leaving yarn A attached, join yarn B and rep rows 5–6. *91 sts*

Break yarn B and continue in yarn A.

Rows 177–186: Rep rows 5–6. *96 sts*

Decrease section

Row 187 (RS): K2, sm, k2tog, k to end. *1 st dec*

Row 188 (WS): Knit.

Rows 189–202: Rep rows 187–188. *88 sts*

Two-color brioche section

Set-up row (RS): Using yarn B, k2, sm, k2tog, *sl1 wyif, yo, k1; rep from * to end. **Do not turn.** Slide sts back to opposite end of needle. *87 sts*

Row 1 (RS): Using yarn A, k2, sl1 wyif, yof, *p2tog, sl1 wyif, yof; rep from * to last 2 sts, p2tog, k1. Turn.

Row 2 (WS): Using yarn B, p1, *sl1 wyif, yof, p2tog; rep from * to last 2 sts, p2. **Do not turn.** Slide sts back to opposite end of needle.

Row 3 (WS): Using yarn A, p1, *k2tog, sl1 wyif, yo; rep from * to last 2 sts, k2. Turn.

Row 4 (RS): Using yarn B, k2, p3tog (working 2 sts and 1 yo), k2tog, *sl1 wyif, yo, k2tog; rep from * to last 2 sts, sl1 wyif, yo, k1. **Do not turn.** Slide sts back to opposite end of needle. *1 st dec*

Row 5 (RS): Using yarn A, k2, p1, sl1 wyif, yof, *p2tog, sl1 wyif, yof; rep from * to last 2 sts, p2tog, k1. Turn.

Row 6 (WS): Using yarn B, p1, *sl1 wyif, yof, p2tog; rep from * to last 3 sts, sl1 wyif, yof, p2. **Do not turn.** Slide sts back to opposite end of needle.

make it yours If you want to add in a second two-color brioche band, try reversing the yarns to create the opposite effect.

tip Try to maintain an even gauge (tension) when working the two-color brioche section so the stitches look neater.

Row 7 (WS): Using yarn A, p1, *k2tog, sl1 wyif, yo; rep from * to last 3 sts, k2tog, k2. Turn.

Row 8 (RS): Using yarn B, k2, k3tog (working 2 sts and 1 yo), *sl1 wyif, yo, k2tog; rep from * to last 2 sts, sl1 wyif, yo, k1. **Do not turn.** Slide sts back to opposite end of needle. *1 st dec*

Row 9 (RS): Using yarn A, k2, sl1 wyif, yof, *p2tog, sl1 wyif, yof; rep from * to last 2 sts, p2tog, k1. Turn.

Row 10 (WS): Using yarn B, p1, *sl1 wyif, yof, p2tog; rep from * to last 2 sts, p2. **Do not turn.** Slide sts back to opposite end of needle.

Row 11 (WS): Using yarn A, p1, *k2tog, sl1 wyif, yo; rep from * to last 2 sts, k2. Turn.

Rows 12–23: Rep rows 4–11, then rows 4–7 only.

Row 24 (RS): Using yarn B, k2, k3tog (working 2 sts and 1 yo), k1, *k2tog, k1; rep from * to end. Turn. *81 sts*

Row 25 (WS): Using yarn B only, k to end. Turn.
Brioche section now complete.
Break yarn A and continue in yarn B only.

Decrease section

Next row (RS): K2, sm, k2tog, k to end. *1 st dec*

Next row (WS): Knit.
Rep last 2 rows a further 77 times. *3 sts*
Bind (cast) off.

making up and finishing

Weave in all loose ends and block to measurements, noting that the garter stitch will spring back on itself again when dry.

tip Brioche knitting is created by knitting a yarn over (yo/yof) and slipped stitch together on the row following the one they were made on. Each brioche row is worked twice; once in yarn A and once in yarn B before turning to work the opposite direction. When worked with two contrasting shades of yarn, brioche knitting gives an eye-catching and bold effect.

skill level

ocean blue

An easy-knit, easy-wear shoulder stole with button detail is the perfect cozy cover up. Accessorize it with treasured or statement buttons for an extra-special touch.

materials

Caron Simply Soft (100% acrylic, approx 315yd/288m per 6oz/170g ball) worsted (Aran) weight yarn
  2 balls of shade Ocean 9759

US 10½ (7mm) knitting needles

Note: There is no direct US conversion for a 7mm needle so if you are unable to find the stated 7mm needle we suggest using US 10½ (6.5mm).

Tapestry needle

3 buttons, 1in (2.5cm) diameter

finished measurements

17in (43cm) wide x 45in (114cm) long

gauge (tension)

14 sts x 20 rows to measure 4in (10cm) over stockinette (stocking) stitch on US 10½ (7mm) needles after blocking

abbreviations

See page 126.

make it yours This simple design is the perfect blank canvas for adding your own colorwork pattern, whether that be stripes, a fancy Fair Isle design, or contrasting textures of yarn.

for the stole

Using US 10½ (7mm) needles, cast on 58 sts.

Row 1 (RS): [K1, p1] to end.

Row 2 (WS): [P1, k1] to end.

Rows 3–4: Rep rows 1–2.

Row 5: [K1, p1] twice, k to last 4 sts, [k1, p1] twice.

Row 6: [P1, k1] twice, p to last 4 sts, [p1, k1] twice.

Rep rows 5–6 until piece measures 43in (109cm) from cast-on edge, or 2in (5cm) less than desired length, ending with a WS row.

Next row (RS)(Buttonholes): [K1, p1] twice, k2, [k2tog, yo, k4] twice, k2tog, yo, k to last 4 sts, [k1, p1] twice.

Next row (WS): [P1, k1] twice, p to last 4 sts, [p1, k1] twice.

Rep rows 5-6 twice more.

Next row (RS): [K1, p1] to end.

Next row (WS): [P1, k1] to end.

Rep last 2 rows once more.

Bind (cast) off knitwise.

making up and finishing

Weave in all loose ends and block to measurements.

With RS facing, lay the shawl flat, with the short edge that has the buttonholes on the left. Sew buttons along the top (long) edge at 8½in (22cm), 10in (25cm), and 11½in (28cm) from the right-hand short edge.

tips The buttonholes here are created with single yarn overs (yo) but if you want to add especially large buttons, work two yarn overs and drop one of the loops as you work back along the row, thus creating a larger hole.

Double check the size of your stole by wrapping it around your shoulders as you work and assess where and when to position the buttonholes as you go.

simply stylish

Stay snug in an ultra cozy, fuss-free shoulder capelet. Worked in the round with a thick but light yarn, this garment knits up quickly and easily when the weather starts to turn wintery.

materials

Lion Brand Wool-Ease Thick & Quick (80% acrylic, 20% wool, approx 106yd/97m per 6oz/170g ball) super-bulky (super-chunky) weight yarn
  4 balls of shade Fisherman 099

US 15 (10mm) circular needles, 16in (40cm), 24in (60cm), and 32in (80cm) lengths

5 stitch markers—1 in a different color/style to the other 4

Tapestry needle

finished measurements

To fit up to 42in (107cm) bust circumference

24in (60cm) long from neckline

gauge (tension)

20 sts x 26 rows to measure 4in (10cm) over stockinette (stocking) stitch on US 15 (10mm) needles in yarn A after blocking

abbreviations

See page 126.

make it yours The simple shape of this cape makes it the perfect canvas for stripes or a more complex Fair Isle colorwork pattern along the lower portion of the garment.

for the cape

Using US 15 (10mm) needles, cast on 54 sts. Join for working in the round, taking care not to twist the sts and place the unique stitch marker to indicate beginning of round.

Rounds 1–21: Knit.

Round 22: Knit and at the same time pm after st 8, 19, 35, and 46. These 4 markers indicate the shoulder increase points.

Round 23: [K to marker, yo, sm, k1, yo] 4 times, k to end. *8 sts inc*

Round 24: Knit.

Rounds 25–34: Rep rounds 23–24. *102 sts*

Round 35: [K to marker, yo, sm, k1, yo] 4 times, k to end. *8 sts inc*

Rounds 36–38: Knit.

Rounds 39–54: Rep rounds 35–38. *142 sts*

Rounds 55–68: Knit.

Bind (cast) off knitwise.

making up and finishing

Weave in all loose ends and block to measurements.

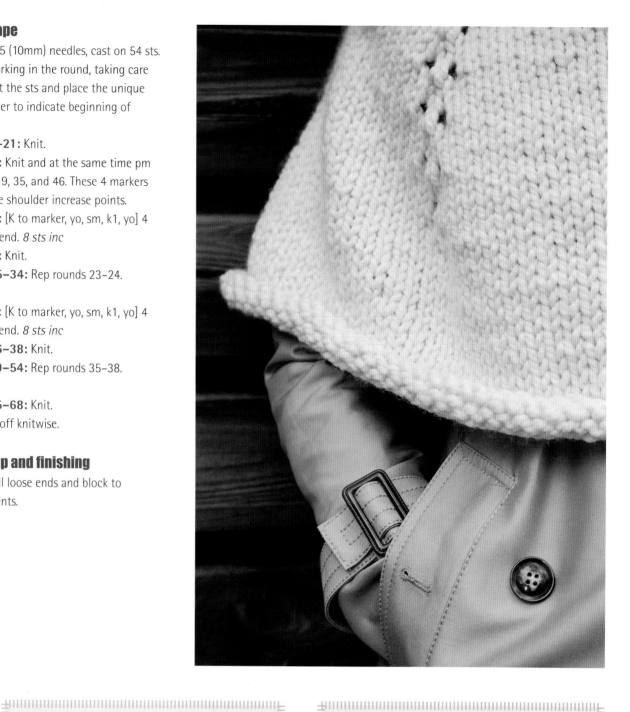

tip Cast on with the shortest circular needle and gradually switch up to the longer lengths as the number of stitches and garment circumference increase.

tip It is vital that the stitches don't twist when joining to work in the round. To ensure they are straight, knit the first row but don't turn at the end so the knit side of the fabric is still facing you, then join the round.

skill level

wood and stone

Surround yourself in this super-sized shawl with a delicate ruffled edging. Worked from the point to the picot bind (cast) off, regular increases are made to create a soft triangular shape. Work in combinations of your favorite colors to make the design your own.

materials

Rowan Summerlite DK (100% cotton, approx 142yd/130m per 1¾oz/50g ball) light worsted (DK) weight yarn

- 2 balls of shade Linen 460 (A)
- 2 balls of shade Plaster 452 (B)
- 2 balls of shade Mushroom 454 (C)
- 3 balls of shade Mocha 451 (D)

US 8 (5mm) circular needle, minimum 60in (150cm) length

Note: The shawl is worked flat in rows but a circular needle is recommended due to the high stitch count.

2 stitch markers

Tapestry needle

finished measurements

94½in (240cm) wide x 43in (109cm) deep

gauge (tension)

14 sts x 20 rows to measure 4in (10cm) over stockinette (stocking) stitch on US 8 (5mm) needles after blocking

abbreviations

See page 126.

for the shawl

Using US 8 (5mm) needles and yarn A, cast on 3 sts.

Row 1 (RS): [K1, yo] twice, k1. *5 sts*

Row 2 (WS): Purl.

Row 3: K1, yo, k to last st, yo, k1. *7 sts*

Row 4: Purl.

Row 5: *[K1, yo] twice, pm; rep from * once more, [k1, yo] twice, k1. *13 sts; 2 markers placed—slip these as you pass them on all subsequent rows*

Row 6: Purl.

Row 7: Knit.

Row 8: Purl.

Row 9: K1, yo, *k to marker, yo, sm, k1, yo; rep from * once more, k to last st, yo, k1. *6 sts inc*

Rows 10–113: Rep rows 6–9. *175 sts*

Rows 114–149: Using yarn B, rep rows 6–9. *229 sts*

Rows 150–185: Using yarn C, rep rows 6–9. *283 sts*

Rows 186–221: Using yarn D, rep rows 6–9. *337 sts*

For the picot bind (cast) off

Using the cable cast-on method (see page 113), cast on 2 sts, immediately bind (cast) off 4 sts, *slip st on RH needle back to LH needle, cable cast on 2 sts, bind (cast) off 4 sts; rep from * to end. Fasten off.

making up and finishing

Weave in all loose ends and block to measurements taking time to pin out the picot points.

---

tip The size and quantity of yarn used for this shawl means it gets quite heavy as you are knitting it. Be sure to rest the project comfortably on your lap to support the weight and take regular breaks to stretch and relax your hands.

tip When changing from one color to the next leave a tail of at least 4in (10cm) so you can weave the ends in neatly when you finish.

make it yours This shawl is knit in a light worsted (DK) weight yarn, however you could make a smaller and finer version by working with a 2ply (lace) weight yarn.

mint julep cowl

This technique for knitting with two colors means that you are slipping stitches then working them in the following round. The simple construction of the cowl means that this is the perfect project for an introduction to two-color brioche knitting.

materials
Berroco Comfort (50% nylon, 50% acrylic, approx 211yd/193m per 3½oz/100g ball) worsted (Aran) weight yarn
   1 ball of shade Aunt Martha Green 9748 (A)
   1 ball of shade Pot Au Feu 9834 (B)

US 8 (5mm) circular needle, 32in (80cm) length

US 9 (5.5mm) circular needle, 32in (80cm) length

Stitch marker

Tapestry needle

finished measurements
45in (115cm) circumference x 10in (25cm) wide

gauge (tension)
14 sts x 38 rows to measure 4in (10cm) over pattern on US 8 (5mm) needles after blocking

abbreviations
See page 126.

special brioche knitting abbreviations
k2tog: Knit the slipped stitch and yarn over next to it together

p2tog: Purl the slipped stitch and yarn over next to it together

sl1 wyif: Slip stitch purlwise with yarn held at front

yo: Take yarn over needle from front to back creating a yarn over

yof: Take yarn over needle from front to back and to the front again, creating a yarn over

for the cowl
Using US 9 (5.5mm) needles and yarn A, cast on 160 sts. Join for working in the round, taking care not to twist the sts and place a stitch marker to indicate beginning of round.
Knit 3 rounds.
Change to US 8 (5mm) needles.
Set-up round: *Sl1 wyif, yo, k1; rep from * to end.
Round 1: *P2tog, sl1, yof; rep from * to end.
Round 2: Sl1 wyif, yo, k2tog, *sl1 wyif, yo, k2tog; rep from * to end.
Round 3: Using yarn B, *p2tog, sl1, yof; rep from * to end.
Round 4: Using yarn A, sl1 wyif, yo, k2tog, *sl1 wyif, yo, k2tog; rep from * to end.

Rep rounds 3–4 until work measures 9in (23cm) ending with round 4.
Break yarn B and continue in yarn A only.
Next round: *P2tog, sl1 wyif, yof; rep from * to end.
Next round: Sl1 wyif, yo, k2tog, *sl1 wyif, yo, k2tog; rep from * to end.
Change to US 9 (5.5mm) needles.
Next round: *K2tog, k1; rep from * to end.
Knit 2 rounds.
Bind (cast) off.

making up and finishing
Weave in all loose ends and block gently to measurements.

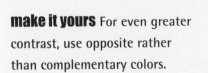

tips It can be tricky to spot and subsequently correct mistakes in brioche knitting, so work through the pattern carefully and place lifelines (see page 8) regularly in case you need to rip back.

Don't break the yarn after working each contrasting round, simply carry the yarn not in use loosely up the inside of the cowl.

make it yours For even greater contrast, use opposite rather than complementary colors.

techniques

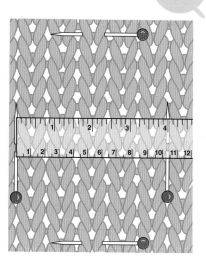

Gauge (tension)

A gauge (tension) is given with each pattern to help you make your item the same size as the sample. The gauge is given as the number of stitches and rows you need to work to produce a 4in (10cm) square of knitting.

Using the recommended yarn and needles, cast on 8 stitches more than the gauge instruction asks for, so if you need to have 10 stitches to 4in (10cm), cast on 18 stitches. Working in pattern as instructed, work eight rows more than is needed. Bind (cast) off loosely.

Lay the swatch flat without stretching it. Lay a ruler across the stitches as shown, with the 2in (5cm) mark centered on the knitting, then put a pin in the knitting at the start of the ruler and at the 4in (10cm) mark: the pins should be well away from the edges of the swatch. Count the number of stitches between the pins. Repeat the process across the rows to count the number of rows to 4in (10cm).

If the number of stitches and rows you've counted is the same as the number asked for in the instructions, you have the correct gauge. If you do not have the same number then you will need to adjust your gauge.

To adjust gauge you need to change the size of your knitting needles—use larger needles to achieve fewer stitches and smaller ones to achieve more stitches.

Holding needles

If you are a knitting novice, you will need to discover which is the most comfortable way for you to hold your needles.

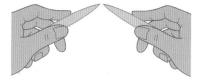

Like a knife

Pick up the needles, one in each hand, as if you were holding a knife and fork—that is to say, with your hands lightly over the top of each needle. As you knit, you will tuck the blunt end of the right-hand needle under your arm, let go with your hand, and use your hand to manipulate the yarn, returning your hand to the needle to move the stitches along.

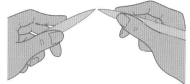

Like a pen

Now try changing the right hand so you are holding the needle as you would hold a pen, with your thumb and forefinger lightly gripping the needle close to its pointed tip and the shaft resting in the crook of your thumb. As you knit, you will not need to let go of the needle but simply slide your right hand forward to manipulate the yarn.

Holding yarn

As you knit, you will be working stitches off the left-hand needle and onto the right-hand needle, and the yarn you are working with needs to be tensioned and manipulated to produce an even fabric. To hold and tension the yarn you can use either your right or left hand, depending on the method you are going to use to make the stitches.

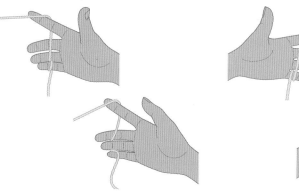

Yarn in right hand

To knit and purl in the US/UK style (see pages 116 and 117), hold the yarn in your right hand. You can wind the yarn around your fingers in different ways, depending on how tightly you need to hold it to achieve an even gauge (tension). Try both ways shown to find out which works best for you.

To hold the yarn tightly (top), wind it right around your little finger, under your ring and middle fingers, then pass it over your index finger, which will manipulate the yarn.

For a looser hold (bottom), catch the yarn between your little and ring fingers, pass it under your middle finger, then over your index finger.

Yarn in left hand

To knit and purl in the continental style (see pages 116 and 117), hold the yarn in your left hand. This method is sometimes easier for left-handed people to use, though many left-handers are quite comfortable knitting with the yarn in their right hand. Try the ways shown to find out which works best for you.

To hold the yarn tightly (top), wind it right around your little finger, under your ring and middle fingers, then pass it over your index finger, which will manipulate the yarn.

For a looser hold (bottom), fold your little, ring, and middle fingers over the yarn, and wind it twice around your index finger.

Making a slipknot

You need to make a slipknot to form the first cast-on stitch.

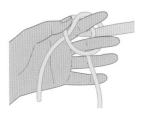 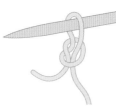

1 With the ball of yarn on your right, lay the end of the yarn on the palm of your left hand and hold it in place with your left thumb. With your right hand, take the yarn around your top two fingers to form a loop. Take the knitting needle through the back of the loop from right to left and use it to pick up the strand nearest to the yarn ball, as shown in the diagram. Pull the strand through to form a loop at the front.

2 Slip the yarn off your fingers, leaving the loop on the needle. Gently pull on both yarn ends to tighten the knot. Then pull on the yarn leading to the ball of yarn to tighten the knot on the needle.

Casting on (cable method)

There are a few methods of casting on for various shawl projects and this one, the cable method, uses two needles.

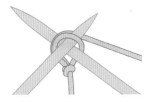  

1 Make a slipknot as shown above. Put the needle with the slipknot into your left hand. Insert the point of the other needle into the front of the slipknot and under the left-hand needle. Wind the yarn from the ball of yarn around the tip of the right-hand needle.

2 Using the tip of the needle, draw the yarn through the slipknot to form a loop. This loop is the new stitch. Slip the loop from the right-hand needle onto the left-hand needle.

3 To make the next stitch, insert the tip of the right-hand needle between the two stitches. Wind the yarn over the right-hand needle, from left to right, then draw the yarn through to form a loop. Transfer this loop to the left-hand needle. Repeat until you have cast on the right number of stitches for the project.

Casting on (backward loop method)

A simple method of casting on stitches where you need to bridge a gap, for example, across a buttonhole. It's shown here worked after a slipknot, but the method is the same if the stitches are being cast on after an existing knitted stitch.

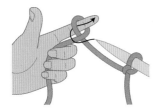 

1 Hold the knitting needle in your right hand. *From front to back, wrap the working yarn around your left index finger. Slip the needle under the loop around your finger in the direction indicated by the arrow.

2 Slide your thumb out of the loop and pull the new stitch tight on the needle. Repeat from * until you have cast on the required number of stitches for the project.

Long-tail cast on

This method only uses one needle, plus finger and thumb. It might look hard to understand at first glance, but once you get the hang of it, it will become intuitive and relatively quick to do. The long-tail cast on produces a neat, stretchy edge suitable for projects that begin with a section of ribbing.

1 Pull out a long tail of yarn, then make a slipknot and put it onto a needle, holding this needle in your dominant hand. Hold your other hand with the palm facing toward you, and wind the long tail of yarn around your thumb in a counterclockwise direction. Pass the other end of the yarn (attached to the ball) over your index finger, as shown. Trap both the strands in place under your third and little finger.

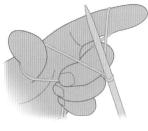

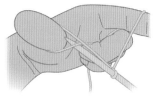

2 Insert your needle under the horizontal strand of yarn that is on the outside of your thumb.

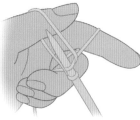

3 Now guide the needle over and then under the strand attached to your index finger, as shown.

4 Bring the needle back through the center of the loop around your thumb to make the stitch.

5 Remove your thumb from the loop and tighten up the stitch by pulling on the long tail. Reposition the yarn around your thumb, as in step 1, and repeat these steps for each cast-on stitch.

Moebius cast on

For the moebius pattern on pages 50–51, you will need a special cast-on method, using circular needles. Instructions are given here, based on Cat Bordhi's video tutorial on Youtube, which you may also find helpful: youtube.com/watch?v=LVnTda7F2V4

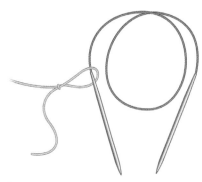

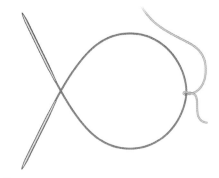

1 Make a slipknot in the working yarn and place on the circular needle.

2 Slide the slipknot to the center of the circular needle cable.

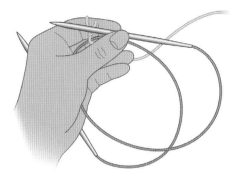

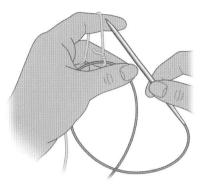

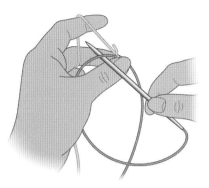

3 Bring the left-hand needle tip around to the slipknot—this will form a loop in the cable of the circular needle.

4 The left-hand needle is held in the right-hand and used to cast on the stitches. Allow the tail of the yarn and the right-hand needle on the cable to hang down. Holding the cable in the left hand, tension the yarn around your index finger.

5 The stitches are alternately cast on to the cable and then the needle tip. Begin by bringing the tip of the needle toward you, then under the loop of the cable.

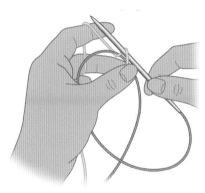

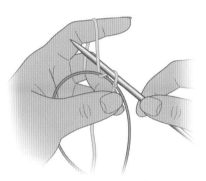

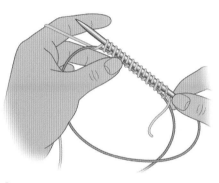

6 Use the tip of the needle to catch the working yarn and bring to the top—this will leave a loop on the needle. First stitch is made.

7 Now bring the working yarn over the tip of the needle to create the next stitch.

8 Repeat steps 5–7 to cast on, only counting the stitches (loops) that sit over the needle.

9 Once the correct number of stitches has been cast on (counting the loops over the needle only), lay the work flat and ease the cable so that the needle tips are in a working position. Slide the stitches carefully around the needle. With the needle flat you will see there is a single twist in the cable.

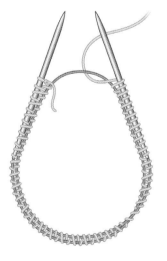

10 With the needle tips brought together to work the stitches, place a stitch marker to indicate the beginning of the round. The twisted, moebius, nature means that you will seemingly work around twice—the upper stitches, then the inner ones—when the stitch marker returns again to the point between the needle this is the start of the next round.

Knit stitch

There are only two stitches to master in knitting; knit and purl. Likewise, there are two main styles of knitting (with a sprinkling of other international techniques); the American/British style and a method referred to as Continental style.

American/British style

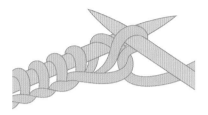

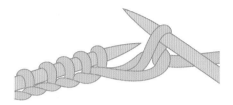

1 Hold the needle with the cast-on stitches in your left hand, and then insert the point of the right-hand needle into the front of the first stitch from left to right. Wind the yarn around the point of the right-hand needle, from left to right.

2 With the tip of the right-hand needle, pull the yarn through the stitch to form a loop. This loop is the new stitch.

3 Slip the original stitch off the left-hand needle by gently pulling the right-hand needle to the right. Repeat these steps until you have knitted all the stitches on the left-hand needle. To work the next row, transfer the needle with all the stitches into your left hand.

Continental style

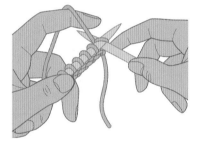

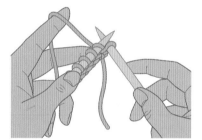

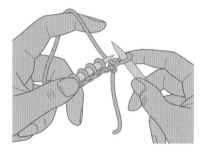

1 Hold the needle with the stitches to be knitted in your left hand, and then insert the tip of the right-hand needle into the front of the first stitch from left to right. Holding the yarn fairly taut with your left hand at the back of your work, use the tip of the right-hand needle to pick up a loop of yarn.

2 With the tip of the right-hand needle, bring the yarn through the original stitch to form a loop. This loop is the new stitch.

3 Slip the original stitch off the left-hand needle by gently pulling the right-hand needle to the right. Repeat these steps until you have knitted all the stitches on the left-hand needle. To work the next row, transfer the needle with all the stitches into your left hand.

Purl stitch

As with knit stitch, purl stitch can be formed in two ways. If you are new to knitting, try both techniques to see which works better for you: left-handed knitters may find the Continental method easier to master.

American/British style

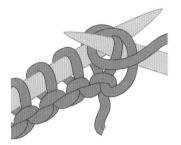  

1 Hold the needle with the stitches in your left hand, and then insert the point of the right-hand needle into the front of the first stitch from right to left. Wind the yarn around the point of the right-hand needle, from right to left.

2 With the tip of the right-hand needle, pull the yarn through the stitch to form a loop. This loop is the new stitch.

3 Slip the original stitch off the left-hand needle by gently pulling the right-hand needle to the right. Repeat these steps until you have purled all the stitches on the left-hand needle. To work the next row, transfer the needle with all the stitches into your left hand.

Continental style

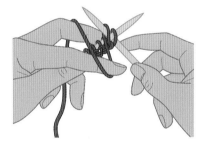  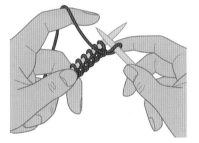

1 Hold the needle with the stitches to be knitted in your left hand, and then insert the tip of the right-hand needle into the front of the first stitch from right to left. Holding the yarn fairly taut at the front of the work, move the tip of the right-hand needle under the working yarn, then push your left index finger downward, as shown, to hold the yarn around the needle.

2 With the tip of the right-hand needle, bring the yarn through the original stitch to form a loop.

3 Slip the original stitch off the left-hand needle by gently pulling the right-hand needle to the right. Repeat these steps until you have purled all the stitches on the left-hand needle. To work the next row, transfer the needle with all the stitches into your left hand.

Binding (casting) off

You need to bind (cast) off the stitches to complete a project and prevent the knitting from unraveling.

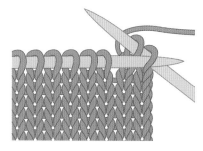

1 First knit two stitches in the usual way. With the point of the left-hand needle, pick up the first stitch you have just knitted and lift it over the second stitch. Knit another stitch so that there are two stitches on the right-hand needle again. Repeat the process of lifting the first stitch over the second stitch. Continue this process until just one stitch remains on the right-hand needle.

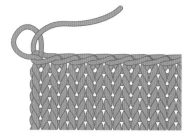

2 Break the yarn, leaving a tail of yarn long enough to sew the work together (see page 124). Pull the tail all the way through the last stitch. Slip the stitch off the needle and pull it fairly tightly to make sure it is secure.

Slipping stitches

Knitwise

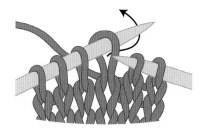

From left to right, put the right-hand needle into the next stitch on the left-hand needle (as shown by the arrow) and slip it across onto the right-hand needle without working it.

Purlwise

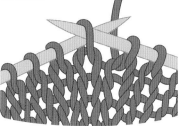

You can slip a stitch purlwise on a purl row or a knit row. From right to left, put the right-hand needle into the next stitch on the left-hand needle and slip it across onto the right-hand needle without working it.

Increasing

There are two methods of increasing used in this book.

Yarn over (yo)

To make a yarn over you wind the yarn around the right-hand needle to make an extra loop that is worked as a stitch on the next row.

To make a yarn over between knit stitches (right) bring the yarn between the tips of the needles to the front. Take the yarn over the right-hand needle to the back and knit the next stitch on the left-hand needle (see page 116).

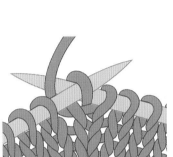

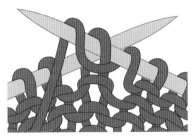

To make a yarn over between purl stitches (above), wrap the yarn over and right around the right-hand needle. Purl the next stitch on the left-hand needle (see page 117).

Knit front and back (kfb)

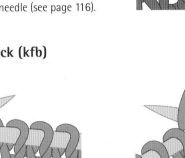

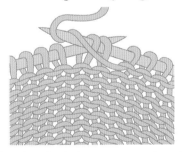

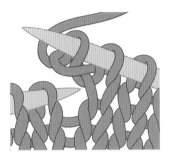

1 Knit the next stitch on the left-hand needle in the usual way (see page 116), but do not slip the "old" stitch off the left-hand needle.

2 Move the right-hand needle behind the left-hand needle and put it into the same stitch again, but through the back of the stitch this time. Knit the stitch again.

3 Now slip the "old" stitch off the left-hand needle in the usual way.

Decreasing

There are five different ways of decreasing used in this book, one of which decreases by two stitches rather than one stitch.

Knit two together (k2tog)

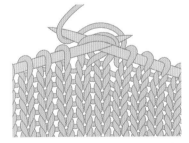

This is the simplest way of decreasing. Simply insert the right-hand needle through two stitches instead of the normal one, and then knit them in the usual way.

The same principle is used to knit three stitches together (k3tog): just insert the right-hand needle through three stitches instead of through two.

Purl two together (p2tog)

To make a simple decrease on a purl row, insert the right-hand needle through two stitches instead of the normal one, and then purl them in the usual way.

The same principle is used to purl three stitches together (p3tog): just insert the right-hand needle through three stitches instead of through two.

Slip, slip, knit (ssk)

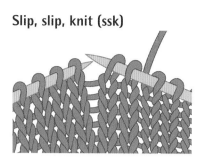

1 Slip one stitch knitwise, and then the next stitch knitwise onto the right-hand needle, without knitting them.

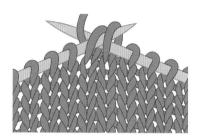

2 Insert the left-hand needle from left to right through the front loops of both the slipped stitches and knit them in the usual way.

Slip 1 stitch, knit 2 stitches together, pass the slipped stitch over (sl1 k2tog psso)

Reduce the number of stitches by two using this decrease.

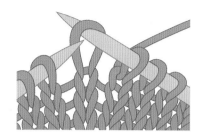

1 Slip the first stitch knitwise from the left-hand needle to the right-hand needle (see left).

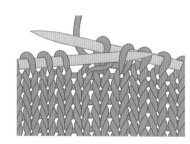

3 Finally, lift the slipped stitch over the knitted stitch and drop it off the needle. You have decreased by two stitches.

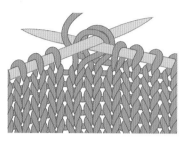

2 Knit the next two stitches on the left-hand needle together (see page 116).

Slip 2 stitches, knit 1 stitch, pass the slipped stitches over (sl2 k1 psso))

Slip 2 stitches knitwise from the left to the right-hand needle (see left). Knit the next stitch as normal, and then pass the two slipped stitches over the knitted stitch and off the right-hand needle.

Knitting in the round

You can knit seamless tubes by working round and round rather than back and forth. There are three ways of doing this, depending on how large the tube needs to be. When working in the round you only work knit stitches (see page 116) to create a stockinette (stocking) stitch fabric.

Circular needles

These needles have short straight tips that are joined with a nylon cable. As well as the usual needle size information, the pattern will tell you what length of needle you need so that your stitches fit on it without stretching.

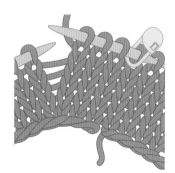

1 Cast on the number of stitches needed (see page 114); just ignore the cable connecting the two tips and cast on the stitches as if you were using two separate needles. Spread out the cast-on row along the length of the cable, making sure the stitches do not become twisted as this will create an unwanted twist in your knitting.

2 Knit the stitches from the right-hand tip onto the left-hand tip, sliding them around the cable as you work. The first stitch is the beginning of the round, so place a round marker on the needle to keep track of the rounds. When you get back to the marker, you have completed one round. Slip the marker onto the right-hand tip of the needle and knit the next round.

Double-pointed needles

If you do not have enough stitches to stretch around a circular needle (see opposite), then you need to work on double-pointed needles. This is one of those knitting techniques that looks terrifying, but isn't actually that hard to do; you just ignore all the needles other than the two you are working with. Double-pointed needles—usually called "DPNs"—come in sets of four or five and a pattern will tell you how many you need.

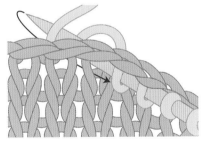

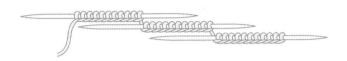

1 Divide evenly into three (if using four needles), or into four (if using five needles), the number of stitches you need to cast on. Here, a set of four needles is being used. Cast on (see page 114) to one needle one-third of the number of stitches needed, plus one extra stitch. Slip the extra stitch onto the second needle. Repeat the process, not forgetting to count the extra stitch, until the right number of stitches is cast on to each of the needles.

2 Arrange the needles in a triangle with the tips overlapping as shown here. As with circular needles (see page 120) make sure that the cast-on edge is not twisted and place a marker to keep track of the beginning of the round. Pull the working tail of yarn across from the last stitch and using the free needle, knit the first stitch off the first needle, knitting it firmly and pulling the yarn tight. Knit the rest of the stitches on the first needle, which then becomes the free one, ready to knit the stitches off the second needle. Knit the stitches off each needle in turn; when you get back to the marker, you have completed one round. Slip the marker onto the next needle and knit the next round.

Picking up stitches

For some projects, you will need to pick up stitches along either the row-end edge or the cast-on/bound- (cast-) off edge of the knitting. The picked-up stitches are shown here in a contrast color for clarity.

Picking up along a row-end edge

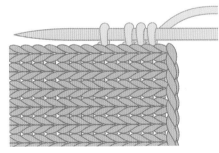

With the right side of the knitting facing you, put a knitting needle from front to back between the first and second stitches of the first row. Wind the yarn around the needle and pull through a loop to form the new stitch. As a knitted stitch is wider than it is tall, you will need to miss out picking up a stitch from about every fourth row in order to make sure the picked-up edge lies flat and even.

Picking up along a cast-on or bound- (cast-) off edge

This is worked in the same way as picking up stitches along a vertical edge, except you will work through the cast-on stitches rather than the gaps between rows. You can pick up one stitch from every existing stitch.

Carrying yarn up the side of the work

When you knit stripe patterns with even numbers of rows in each color, you do not need to break the yarn and weave it in at the end of each stripe. You can carry the color not in use up the side of the work until you need it again.

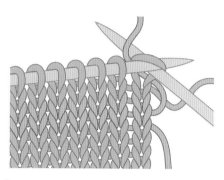

1 If the stripes change every two rows, then just bring the yarn not in use up and knit with it as needed.

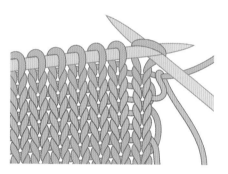

2 If the stripes are deeper, then you need to catch in the yarn not in use at the ends of rows to prevent long, loose strands appearing. To do this, put the right-hand needle into the first stitch of a row, lay the yarn to be carried over the working yarn, and then knit the stitch in the working yarn.

Weaving in ends

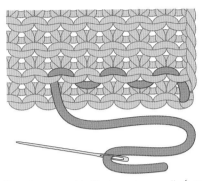

Use a large-eyed knitter's sewing needle (or a tapestry needle), which has a blunt tip to weave the yarn end in and out of a few stitches—the end is shown here in a contrast color for clarity.

Blocking

If, once you have finished the piece of knitting, it doesn't look as smooth and even as you hoped it would, then blocking it can help. You can also use this process to straighten or to re-shape pieces a little if need be. The precise method of blocking you use depends on the fiber the yarn is spun from: the ball band will give you advice on that.

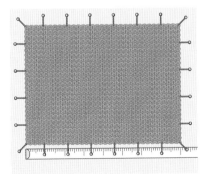

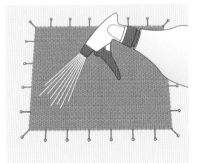

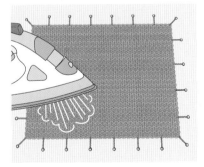

1 Lay the piece of knitting flat on an ironing board and ease it into shape. Don't pull hard and keep the knitting flat. Starting at the corners (if there are any), pin the edges of the piece to the ironing board, pushing the pins in far enough to hold the knitting firmly. Use a ruler or tape measure to check that the pinned pieces are the right size.

2 If the fiber or texture of your yarn does not respond well to heat, then use a spray bottle of cold water to completely dampen the knitting, but do not make it soaking wet. Let the knitting dry naturally, then unpin it.

3 If you can use heat, then set the iron to the temperature the yarn ball band recommends. Hold the iron 1in (2.5cm) above the surface of the knitting and steam it for a couple of minutes. Move the iron so that the whole surface gets steamed, but don't actually touch the knitting with the iron as this can spoil the texture and drape of the fabric and may leave shiny patches. Let the knitting dry naturally before unpinning it.

Joining seams with mattress stitch

Mattress stitching row-end edges
The seam is worked from the right side and will be almost invisible.

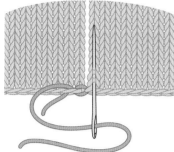 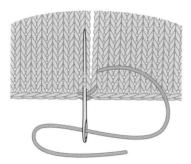 

1 Lay the two edges to be joined side by side, right side up. Thread a knitter's sewing needle with a long length of yarn. From the back bring the needle up between the first and second stitches of the left-hand piece, immediately above the cast-on edge. Take it across to the right-hand piece, and from the back bring it through between the first and second stitches of that piece, immediately above the cast-on edge. Take it back to the left-hand piece and, again from the back, bring it through one row above where it first came through, between the first and second stitches. Pull the yarn through and this figure-eight will hold the cast-on edges level.

2 *Take the needle across to the right-hand piece and, from the front, take it under the bars of yarn between the first and second stitches on the next two rows up. Take the needle across to the left-hand piece and, from the front, take it under the bars of yarn between the first and second stitches on the next two rows up.

3 Repeat from * to sew up the seam. When you have sewn about 1in (2.5cm), gently and evenly pull the stitches tight to close the seam, and then continue.

Mattress stitching cast-on or bound- (cast-) off edges
You can either gently pull the sewn stitches taut but have them visible, as shown, or you can pull them completely tight so that they disappear.

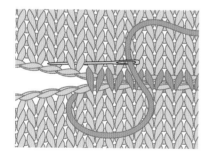 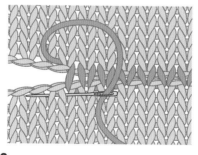

1 Right-sides up, lay the two edges to be joined side by side. Thread a knitters sewing needle with a long length of yarn. Secure the yarn on the back of the lower knitted piece, then bring the needle up through the middle of the first whole stitch in that piece. Take the needle under both loops of the first whole stitch on the upper piece, so that it comes to the front between the first and second stitches.

2 *Go back into the lower piece and take the needle through to the back where it first came out, and then bring it to the front again in the middle of the next stitch along. Pull the yarn through. Take the needle under both loops of the next whole stitch on the upper piece. Repeat from * to sew the seam.

Basic crochet techniques

Making a slipknot

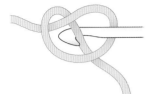 

1 Make a loop of yarn with the tail end going under the circle. With a crochet hook, pull a loop of yarn through the circle.

2 Slip the loop along the hook and pull the tail gently to make a loose loop on the back.

Chain

1 Wrap the yarn over (round) the hook ready to pull it through the loop on the hook.

2 Pull the yarn through, creating a new loop on the hook. Continue in this way to create a chain of the required number of stitches.

Slip stitch

A slip stitch doesn't create any height. It can be used to move to a different position in the work, or to join elements together.

1 Insert the hook into the work as directed, yarn over (round) hook.

2 Pull the yarn through both the work and the loop on the hook at the same time, so that there is just one loop left on the hook.

US single crochet (UK double crochet)

1 Insert the hook into the work as directed, yarn over (round) hook, and pull the yarn through the work only (2 loops on hook).

2 Yarn over (round) hook again, and pull the yarn through the two loops on the hook (1 loop on hook). One stitch completed.

US double crochet (UK treble crochet)

1 Wrap the yarn over (round) the hook before inserting the hook into the work as directed. Put the hook through the work, yarn over (round) hook again and pull through the work (3 loops on hook).

2 Yarn over (round) hook again, pull the yarn through the first 2 loops on the hook (2 loops on hook).

3 Yarn over (round) hook again, and pull the yarn through the 2 loops on the hook, leaving 1 loop on the hook. One stitch completed.

abbreviations and suppliers

abbreviations and US/UK terms

[ ]	work instructions between square brackets as directed
* / **	work instructions after/between asterisk(s) as directed
approx	approximately
bind off (US)	cast off (UK)
ch	chain
dc	double crochet (UK treble crochet)
gauge (US)	tension (UK)
inc	Increase(d)(ing)
k	knit
k2tog	knit 2 stitches together (decrease 1)
kfb	knit into the front then back of one stitch (increase 1)
LH	left-hand
psso	pass slipped stitch(es) over
pm	place marker
p	purl
p2tog	purl 2 stitches together (decrease 1)
rep	repeat
RH	right-hand
RS	right side
sc	single crochet (UK double crochet)
sl	slip
sl1 k2tog psso	slip 1 stitch knitwise, knit next 2 stitches together, pass slipped stitch over the knitted stitch (decrease 2)
sl2 k1 psso	slip 2 stitches together knitwise, knit next stitch, pass slipped stitches over the knitted stitch (decrease 2)
sm	slip marker
ssk	slip 1 stitch knitwise, slip the next stitch knitwise, knit both these stitches together through the back loop
st(s)	stitch(es)
tbl	through the back loop
tog	together
tr	treble crochet (US double crochet)
WS	wrong side
wyif	with yarn in front
yo	yarn over needle and into working position

yarn supplies

Selecting just the right yarn for your make is one of the most satisfying elements of working on a new project—deciding on the fiber, weight, color, and texture—whether you are shopping for something specific or simply picking items from your stash. These wraps and shawls have been created using a selection of different types, styles, and shades of yarn. Here is a selection of suppliers of the sumptuous yarns used in the designs in this book.

Berroco
www.berroco.com
www.loveknitting.com

Brown Sheep Company
www.brownsheep.com
www.loveknitting.com

Cascade
www.cascadeyarns.com
www.loveknitting.com

Caron
www.loveknitting.com
www.yarnspirations.com

Debbie Bliss
www.designeryarns.uk.com
www.knittingfever.com
www.loveknitting.com

Fyberspates
www.fyberspates.com
www.loveknitting.com

GGH
www.loveknitting.com

Katia
www.loveknitting.com
www.knittingfever.com

Lion Brand
www.lionbrand.com
www.loveknitting.com

Malabrigo
www.malabrigoyarn.com
www.loveknitting.com

Noro
www.designeryarns.uk.com
www.knittingfever.com
www.loveknitting.com

Rowan
www.knitrowan.com
www.loveknitting.com
www.jimmybeanswool.com

Schachenmayr
www.loveknitting.com

index

acknowledgments

I love to knit and have had a fabulous time working on all the different shawls for this book—I hope that you have just as much fun creating your own personal collection of wraps and shawls! Over the last few months I feel as though I have never not been knitting, and I can't think of many better ways to spend my day. Thank you for the support and encouragement from my online friends and readers of www.madepeachy.com.

As ever, thank you to Cindy Richards, Penny Craig, Sally Powell, and the team at CICO Books. Huge thanks to Rachel Atkinson and Jemima Bicknell for keeping the patterns on the right track and to the photographers Emma Mitchell and Penny Wincer, stylists Rob Merrett and Joanna Thornhill, and designer Alison Fenton for making this book so beautiful.

I would like to extend my thanks to the companies that supported this book with wonderful yarns, because nothing makes a knitter happier than being surrounded by the finest yarns available! Thanks to Brown Sheep Yarns, Cascade Yarns, Designer Yarns, Fyberspates, Love Knitting, and Rowan—your generosity is hugely appreciated.

To my husband, John, thank you for never losing your patience with the sheer volume of yarn in our home at any given time, and always being on hand to motivate and encourage me—you are the best!